Gifts from the Kitchen

Gifts from the Kitchen

ANNIE RIGG

PHOTOGRAPHY BY CATHERINE GRATWICKE

KYLE BOOKS

Published in 2011
by Kyle Books
www.kylebooks.com

Distributed by National Book
Network
4501 Forbes Blvd., Suite 200
Lanham, MD 20706
Phone: (800) 462-6420; Fax:
(301) 429-5746
custserv@nbnbooks.com

First published in Great Britain in
2010 by Kyle Books

ISBN: 978-1-906868-57-4

Text © 2010 Annie Rigg
Design © 2010 Kyle Cathie Limited

Photography © 2010
Catherine Gratwicke
pp. 10–11, 20–21, 43, 48
Laura Edwards

Editor Judith Hannam
Designer Rashna Mody Clark
Copy Editor Annie Lee
Food Stylist Annie Rigg
Prop Stylist Cynthia Inions
Proofreader Abi Waters
Index Hilary Bird
Production Gemma John

Annie Rigg is hereby identified
as the author of this work in
accordance with section 77
of the Copyright, Designs and
Patents Act 1988.

Library of Congress Control
Number: 2011926469

Printed in Singapore by Tien
Wah Press

Contents

Introduction

Homemade gifts are those that are given with an extra ounce or two of love, a spoonful of originality and a jar-full of creativity. But homemade foodie gifts double those magic ingredients and tie them all up with a fancy ribbon.

There is a food gift for just about every occasion whether it be a birthday, Valentine's Day, Mother's Day or simply to welcome someone into their new home.

Some gifts aren't necessarily everyday food. Fortune cookies, each filled with a personal message, candy-striped bags of light-as-a-feather marshmallows and pastel-colored Love Heart sugar cubes are purely for the joy and laughs that they'll bring and would be perfect for bridal showers and weddings.

Receiving a box of homemade cookies is sure to brighten anyone's day and make the world seem a better place. So let no occasion pass unnoticed and imagine how fabulous it would be to give a box of the richest brownies or a tin of the stickiest, salted caramels for no particular reason, just simply because it's Friday, the sun is shining and you love someone. Any gift would be all the more special if you were able to grow or pick some of the ingredients yourself. A bumper crop of tomatoes can be turned into the most delicious chutney, an abundance of homegrown strawberries or a basket of windfall apples can be transformed into preserves, cordial or jelly. And no walk in the countryside is without its rewards, whether that be picking rose petals, juicy blackberries, damsons or apples that can be infused in gin or turned into jams. For an extra touch, label your jars and preserves, not only with their contents but the day and location of the harvest.

Marmalade, seasonal jams and jellies can be made when the produce is at its very best and most plentiful. Squirrel the jars away in a dark cupboard or cellar so that they are ready to bring out throughout the year or whenever the need arises.

Some gifts will need a little forward planning—flavored vodkas or pickles need time to mature so if you're planning to give them away immediately, be sure to attach instructions for serving and storing.

It isn't just about what you make, it's about the presentation too. Look out for pretty vintage tins, boxes and baskets. Keep a good supply of gift tags and beautiful ribbons in all the colors of the rainbow so that every tray of cookies or candies can be dressed up to the nines. Collect jars, bottles and boxes throughout the year so that they are always on hand to be filled with your homemade delights.

IMAGINE HOW
FABULOUS IT
WOULD BE TO
GIVE A BOX
OF THE MOST
COLORFUL
MACAROONS
OR A TIN OF THE
STICKIEST, SALTED
CARAMELS FOR
NO PARTICULAR
REASON – JUST
SIMPLY BECAUSE
IT'S FRIDAY, THE
SUN IS SHINING
AND YOU LOVE
SOMEONE.

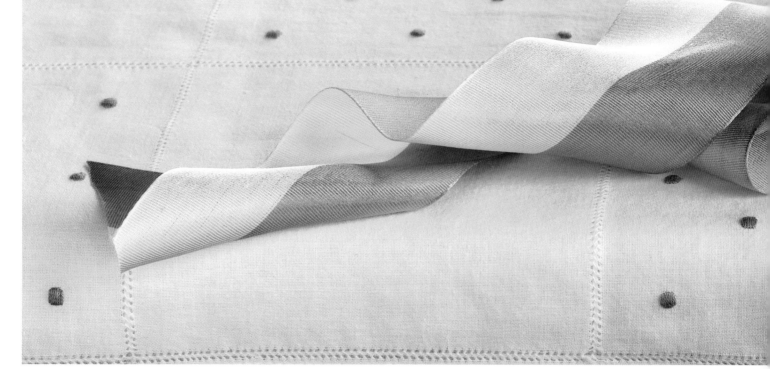

SPRING

CHAPTER 1

Turkish Delight

Pour the sugar into a medium-size saucepan and add the lemon juice and 1¼ cups of water. Stir over low heat to dissolve the sugar, then bring gently to a boil.

Mix the gelatin with ½ cup of the cornstarch and ¾ cup and 2 tablespoons water and add to the saucepan. Stir constantly until the gelatin has dissolved, then continue to simmer very gently for 20 minutes until thickened.

Mix together the remaining cornstarch and the confectioners' (icing) sugar. Lightly oil a 8in. (20cm) square baking pan with a depth of 1½–2in. (4–5cm) and line it with plastic wrap. Lightly dust the plastic wrap with some of the cornstarch mixture, tipping out the excess.

Remove the saucepan from the heat and let cool. Add the rosewater, food-coloring, and pistachios and pour the mixture into the baking pan. Spread level and let cool for at least 4 hours or until completely set before cutting into squares and dusting with the rest of the sugar cornstarch mixture.

 Stored in an airtight container, these will keep for about a week.

MAKES 20 PIECES

1⅔ cups superfine sugar

juice of 1 lemon

4 packets powdered gelatin (1oz/25g in total)

⅔ cup cornstarch

¼ cup confectioners' (icing) sugar

2–3 teaspoons rosewater

pink food-coloring paste

generous ⅓ cup shelled unsalted pistachios, roughly chopped

sunflower oil, for brushing the saucepan

Homemade candies are always a pleasure to make and to receive. A box of sugar-dusted, rose-scented Turkish Delight is something we often associate with Christmas but would make a perfect Valentine's or Mother's Day gift packed into a box lined with waxed paper.

You could also try adding pure lemon extract and a drop of yellow food color in place of the rosewater and pink coloring.

Coffee and Cardamom Toffee

There is something quite nostalgic and old-fashioned about toffee, but here it is given a contemporary twist with coffee and a hint of cardamom.

Brush the inside of a 6¾in. (17cm) square baking pan with sunflower oil.

Place all the ingredients except the cardamom pods in a medium-size saucepan and add ⅓ cup water. Crack the cardamom pods using a mortar and pestle; remove the green husks and finely grind the little black seeds. Add to the saucepan and place over a low to medium heat. Stir to melt the butter and completely dissolve the sugars.

When the sugars have dissolved, raise the heat slightly and bring the mixture to a boil, stirring from time to time. Continue to cook steadily until the toffee registers 260°F (126°C) on a candy thermometer (hard ball stage).

Remove the saucepan from the heat, give the toffee a quick whisk, and pour into the greased baking pan. Let cool and harden before breaking into pieces and packaging in waxed paper.

 Stored in an airtight container, the toffee will keep for about a week.

MAKES ABOUT 20 PIECES

sunflower oil, for brushing the saucepan

1⅛ sticks unsalted butter, diced

scant cup superfine sugar

¾ cup molasses sugar

2 rounded tablespoons corn syrup

2 teaspoons instant coffee granules

½ teaspoon ground cinnamon

pinch of salt

5–6 cardamom pods

Nougat with Cherries and Toasted Marcona Almonds

I have suggested using orange blossom-scented honey for this nougat but you could just as easily use any good-quality, fragrant variety. You could also swap the almonds for blanched, toasted hazelnuts and dried figs and cranberries for the cherries and apricots. Make the nougat the day before you plan on eating it so that it has plenty of time to harden and set.

Preheat the oven to 350°F (180°C). Lightly grease a 6in. (15cm) square pan with a depth of 2in. (5cm), and line the base and sides with a sheet of rice paper.

Lightly toast the almonds and pistachios on a baking sheet in the oven until pale golden brown. Remove from the oven, let cool, then roughly chop. Cut the cherries in half, place them into a sifter, and rinse under cold running water. Dry well on paper towels. Roughly chop the dried apricots.

Place the honey, superfine sugar, and water in a medium saucepan. Set the saucepan over a medium heat, stirring occasionally until the sugar has dissolved. Increase the heat, bring the mixture to a boil, and continue to cook for about 10 minutes, until it reaches 327°F (164°C) on a candy thermometer. Remove the saucepan from the heat.

Whisk the egg white with a pinch of salt in a large heatproof bowl until it holds soft peaks—I recommend a stand mixer as it will make the process a lot easier. Continue to whisk while adding the hot honey caramel mixture in a steady stream. Keep whisking until the mixture stiffens, thickens, and turns pale cream-colored. Add the nuts and dried fruit and stir to combine. Spoon into the prepared pan and spread level. Press another sheet of rice paper on top and let cool.

Once cold, turn the nougat out on to a board and cut into pieces.

 Package in small quantities in transparent cellophane bags. Stored in an airtight container, the nougat will keep for 4–5 days.

MAKES ABOUT 20 SQUARES

- 2 large sheets of edible rice paper
- ⅔ cup blanched Marcona almonds
- generous ⅓ cup shelled, unsalted pistachios
- scant ½ cup natural colored candied cherries
- ⅓ cup dried apricots
- ½ cup orange blossom honey
- 1⅓ cups superfine sugar
- 2 tablespoons water
- 1 large egg white
- pinch of salt

Pink and White Vanilla Marshmallows

Homemade marshmallows are the stuff of dreams! They are light as pink fluffy clouds, oh-so-sweet, and with just a hint of pure vanilla extract. Cut into squares and package into pretty pink- and white-striped bags for bridal showers and girly birthday parties.

Mix the confectioners' (icing) sugar and cornstarch in a small bowl. Lightly grease a 9in. (23cm) square pan with a depth of about 2in. (5cm) with a little sunflower oil and dust with the confectioners' (icing) sugar and cornstarch mix, tapping out and reserving the excess.

Measure 6 tablespoons of cold water into another small bowl, sprinkle over the gelatin and set aside.

Pour the sugar into a medium-size saucepan, add 1 cup water and the corn syrup and place the saucepan over a medium heat until the sugar has dissolved. Bring the mixture to a boil and continue to cook steadily until the syrup reaches 250°F (120°C) on a candy thermometer. Remove from the heat, add the gelatin and stir until thoroughly combined and the gelatin has melted.

Place the egg whites in the bowl of an electric mixer equipped with a whisk attachment. Add a pinch of salt and whisk until the whites hold a stiff peak. Add the vanilla and the hot gelatin syrup in a steady stream and continue to whisk for a further 3–4 minutes, until the mixture will hold a ribbon trail when the beaters are lifted from the bowl.

Pour half the mixture into the prepared saucepan in an even layer. Add a tiny amount of pink food coloring paste to the remaining mixture and stir until evenly colored. Pour the pink marshmallow over the white and let set (at least 2 hours).

Once the marshmallow has completely set, dust the work surface or a board with the remaining confectioners' (icing) sugar and cornstarch mixture. Carefully turn the marshmallow out on to the prepared board and cut into squares, using a sharp knife. Dust the individual marshmallows before packaging.

Package in striped paper bags.
Stored in an airtight box, the marshmallow will keep for 3 days.

MAKES ABOUT 30

1 tablespoon confectioners' (icing) sugar
1 tablespoon cornstarch
sunflower oil, for greasing
2 tablespoons powdered gelatin
2 cups granulated sugar
2½ tablespoons corn syrup
2 large egg whites
pinch of salt
1 teaspoon vanilla extract
pink food coloring paste

Lollipops

Use food-coloring pastes to tint these lollipops whatever shade you desire. The colors are stronger, more varied, and each little pot seems to last forever. If you can't get a hold of a lollipop mold, try setting the lollipops in very well-greased round cutters or flan rings placed on a sheet of parchment paper. Remove the rings just before the lollipops set solid, and firmly press a lollipop stick into each one. Or you could try making them free-form for a more homemade look!

Grease a 6-hole lollipop mold with sunflower oil and line the bottom of each hole with a heart shape of greased parchment paper.

Pour the sugar and syrup into a small saucepan. Add the cream of tartar and ¾ cup of water. Set the saucepan over a gentle heat and warm slowly until the sugar has dissolved. Bring to a steady boil and continue to cook for about 10 minutes, until it reaches the "hard crack" stage, 310°F (154°C) on a candy thermometer. Immediately remove from the heat and add the peppermint or lemon extract, swirling the saucepan to mix in evenly.

Pour roughly three-quarters of the mixture into a small warmed bowl and the rest into another. Add one of the food colorings to the larger quantity and the other to the smaller amount. Stir quickly until each mixture is evenly colored.

Spoon the first mixture into the greased lollipop molds. Drizzle with the second mixture and lightly swirl the two together using a wooden skewer. Place a lollipop stick into each lolly and let set until solid and completely cold before removing from the molds.

Wrap individually in cellophane.
The lollipops are best eaten on the day of making.

MAKES 6 LOLLIPOPS

sunflower oil, for greasing
1½ cups granulated sugar
½ cup golden syrup
½ rounded teaspoon cream of tartar
2 teaspoons peppermint or lemon extract
2 contrasting food coloring pastes

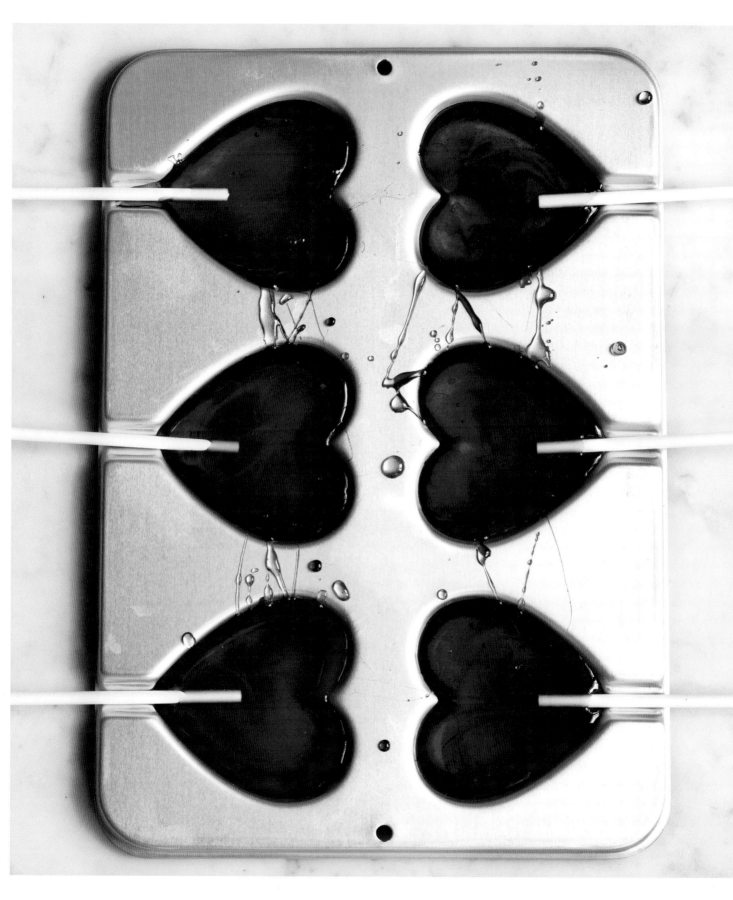

Macaroons

Preheat the oven to 325°F (170°C) and line 2 baking sheets with nonstick parchment paper.

Sift the confectioners' (icing) sugar and ground almonds together into a bowl.

Place the egg whites in the bowl of a stand mixer fitted with a whisk attachment. Add the salt and whisk until the egg whites form soft peaks. Add the superfine sugar a teaspoon at a time, whisking well after each addition. Continue whisking until the mixture is stiff and glossy.

Add the food coloring paste, using the point of a wooden skewer and mixing well to color the mixture evenly.

Fit a pastry bag with a ½in. (1cm) plain tip and pipe 2in. (5cm) disks on to the parchment paper. Dampen the tip of your finger and gently flatten the top of any macaroons that are peaky, then give the sheet a sharp tap on the work surface to knock out air bubbles. Set aside for 30 minutes to allow the mixture to settle, then bake on the middle shelf of the preheated oven for 9–10 minutes.

Remove from the oven and let cool on the sheet.

Once completely cold, sandwich the macaroons together with jam, cream, buttercream, or ganache and serve.

MAKES ABOUT 20 MACAROONS

1¼ cups confectioners' (icing) sugar
½ cup ground almonds
2 large egg whites
pinch of salt
2½ tablespoons superfine sugar
pink, green, yellow, or lilac food coloring paste

Package up in brightly colored boxes, tied with a ribbon. Once filled, the macaroons can be kept in the fridge for a couple of days.

Making these delicate macaroons can become seriously addictive—there is no end to the color and flavor varieties you can create. Use food coloring pastes rather than the liquid variety to tint the macaroon shells, a small pot will color hundreds of macaroons and the selection of colors now available is vast.

Sandwich the macaroons with any number of fillings to match the colors—lemon curd, jam, buttercream, or ganache are all perfect.

Chocolate and Cinnamon Swirl Meringues
and Pink Raspberry Swirl Meringues

Chocolate and Cinnamon Swirl Meringues

These meringues are big, pillowy sugary treats. The method of adding hot sugar to the egg whites means that once cooked the insides of the meringues stay chewy and marshmallowy while the outside is crisp.

Preheat the oven to 400°F (200°C) and line a large, solid baking sheet with nonstick parchment paper.

Pour the sugar into a small roasting pan and place in the preheated oven for about 7 minutes, or until the sugar is hot to the touch. Meanwhile, place the egg whites in the bowl of a stand mixer fitted with a whisk attachment. Add the salt and whisk until frothy.

Turn the oven down to 225°F (110°C).

Quickly pour all the hot sugar on to the egg whites in one go and continue to whisk on high speed for 8–10 minutes, until the meringue mixture is very stiff, white, and cold.

In a small bowl mix together the cocoa and cinnamon. Pour the cocoa mixture into the meringue and, using a large metal spoon, very lightly fold in, using two or three strokes. The trick is to keep the mixture quite marbled in appearance.

Spoon the mixture on to the prepared baking sheet in 4 or 6 equal-size, peaky meringues. Cook on the middle rack of the preheated oven for 1½–1¾ hours, or until dry and crisp. Remove from the oven and let cool on the baking sheet.

Package in cellophane bags tied with a contrasting ribbon and a label with serving instructions—the meringues are delicious eaten on their own or with lightly whipped heavy cream and maybe a scattering of raspberries. They will keep for 3–4 days in an airtight box.

MAKES 4–6 LARGE MERINGUES

1¾ cups superfine sugar

4–5 large egg whites, weighing 5½oz (150g)

pinch of salt

2 tablespoons cocoa

1 teaspoon ground cinnamon

Pink Raspberry Swirl Meringues

Package these large clouds of raspberry swirled meringues in individual boxes lined with paper or in cellophane bags.
They are delicious eaten on their own or with a generous spoonful of softly whipped heavy cream and a handful of fresh raspberries.

MAKES 4–6 LARGE MERINGUES

1⅓ cups superfine sugar

4–5 large egg whites, weighing 5½oz (150g)

pinch of salt

½ teaspoon red food-coloring paste

2 tablespoons raspberry flavoring, optional

3–4 tablespoons (1oz/25g) freeze-dried raspberries

FOR PISTACHIO AND COCONUT MERINGUES

½ cup shredded coconut

generous ⅓ cup unsalted and shelled pistachio nuts, finely chopped

Preheat the oven to 400°F (200°C) and line a solid baking sheet with nonstick parchment paper.

Put the sugar into a small roasting pan and heat in the preheated oven for about 7 minutes, or until hot to the touch.

Place the egg whites and salt in the bowl of a stand mixer and whisk until light and foamy. Remove the hot sugar from the oven and turn the temperature down to 225°F (110°C). Quickly pour the sugar on to the egg whites and whisk on medium speed for 8–10 minutes, until the meringue is very stiff, white, and cold.

Using a wooden skewer, dot the food coloring and drizzle the raspberry flavoring over the meringue mixture, then scatter over the raspberries. Using a large metal spoon, very lightly fold in, using 3 or 4 strokes of the spoon, so that the meringue is marbled with pink.

Spoon the mixture on to the prepared baking sheet in 4–6 large peaky meringue shapes, and bake on the middle rack of the preheated oven for 1½–1¾ hours, or until crisp. Remove from the oven and let cool on the baking sheet.

 Package in pretty boxes or cellophane bags. See serving suggestions opposite. They will keep for 3 days in an airtight box.

VARIATION:

Pistachio and Coconut Meringues

Make up the basic meringue, then add the shredded coconut and the pistachios and fold in, using a large metal spoon. Divide the meringue into 4–6 even-size portions and place on the baking sheet. Cook in the preheated oven for 1½–1¾ hours, then remove from the oven and let cool on the baking sheet.

Raspberry and Rose Chocolate Wafers

Line 2 large baking sheets with nonstick parchment paper.

Break the dark and white chocolate into pieces and melt separately in heatproof bowls set over saucepans of barely simmering water. Stir until smooth, remove from the heat, and cool slightly. Spoon heaping teaspoonfuls of melted chocolate on to the prepared baking sheets, spreading the chocolate into disks with the back of the spoon. Scatter with the raspberries, rose petals, and rose chips or sugar sprinkles.

Set aside to cool and harden completely before removing from the parchment with a round-bladed knife.

 Stored in an airtight container, these will keep for 4–5 days.

MAKES ABOUT 24 WAFERS

5½oz (150g) best-quality dark chocolate (72% cacoa)

5½oz (150g) best-quality white chocolate

3–4 tablespoons freeze-dried raspberries (approx. 1oz/25g)

3–4 tablespoons candied rose petals

3–4 tablespoons pink sugared rose chips or sugar sprinkles

A box of these chocolate wafers would make an ideal gift for Mother's Day—they are easy enough for little hands to make as the only cooking required is to melt the chocolate.

Freeze-dried raspberries are available online or from selected food stores. As an alternative you could top the chocolate wafers with candied stem ginger or chopped dried fruits and nuts.

Chocolate and Hazelnut Madeleines

Light, buttery madeleines are almost begging to be served on the most delicate chinaware and at the most sophisticated tea party. They are cooked in special shell-shaped baking pans that are available in a variety of designs.

Preheat the oven to 350°F (180°C).

Melt the butter either in a small saucepan or in a heatproof bowl in the microwave. Brush the insides of 2 madeleine pans with a little of the melted butter and then lightly dust them with all-purpose flour, knocking out the excess flour by sharply tapping the pans on the work surface.

Sift the flour, baking powder, cocoa, ground hazelnuts, and salt together into a large bowl.

Whisk the eggs, sugar, and honey in a separate large bowl until they have doubled in volume, are very pale and thick, and will hold a ribbon trail when the whisk is lifted from the mixture. Very gently fold in the sifted dry ingredients until only just incorporated. Add the remaining melted butter and gently fold this into the batter, trying not to knock out too much air from the mixture.

Spoon the mixture into the prepared pans, filling them three-quarters full. Bake on the middle shelf of the preheated oven for 10–12 minutes, until well risen and spongy.

Allow the madeleines to rest in the pans for 30 seconds, then turn them out on to wire racks and let cool.

MAKES ABOUT 20 MADELEINES

⅞ **stick unsalted butter**
¾ **cup all-purpose flour, plus extra for dusting**
½ **teaspoon baking powder**
1 **tablespoon cocoa**
⅓ **cup ground hazelnuts**
pinch of salt
2 **large eggs**
⅓ **cup superfine sugar**
1 **tablespoon honey**
confectioners' (icing) sugar, to serve

Package in single layers in between parchment paper in pretty boxes or tins. They will keep for 2–3 days in an airtight box. Dust with confectioners' (icing) sugar to serve.

Greek Honey Cookies

Try to use a deeply fragrant blossom honey for these pine nut-topped cookies. Package in individual cellophane or paper bags or even empty CD or DVD envelopes which have a clever cellophane cut-out on the front, allowing the cookies to be seen.

MAKES ABOUT 20 COOKIES

2 cups all-purpose flour
1 teaspoon baking powder
2 teaspoons baking soda
1 teaspoon ground cinnamon
pinch of ground cloves
¼ cup superfine sugar
pinch of salt
1⅛ sticks unsalted butter, chilled and diced
finely grated zest of 1 orange
⅓ cup clear orange blossom or other fragrant honey
½ cup pine nuts
1 tablespoon honey, to finish

Preheat the oven to 350°F (180°C) and line 2 baking sheets with nonstick parchment paper.

Sift the flour, baking powder, baking soda, cinnamon, cloves, sugar, and salt into a large mixing bowl. Add the butter and rub into the dry ingredients using the tips of your fingers. You can do this in a food processor if you like. Add the orange zest and mix well.

Warm the honey in a small saucepan until runny but not hot. Pour into the dry ingredients and mix well until smooth and thoroughly combined, and the dough comes together into a ball.

Break off double teaspoon-sized nuggets of the cookie dough, roll into balls, and flatten slightly. Arrange on the prepared baking sheets, leaving plenty of space between them, and press a few pine nuts on to the top of each cookie. Bake on the middle rack of the preheated oven for around 12 minutes, or until crisp and golden brown.

Leave on the baking sheets until cold, then lightly brush the tops of the warm cookies with a little honey and leave on the baking sheets until cold.

 Stored in airtight boxes or cookie tins, they will keep for 4–5 days.

Candied Citrus Peel

This recipe makes enough candied peel to make up a number of small gifts. They are delicious eaten just as they are or you could take them to the next level and half dip them in very dark melted chocolate. Or for the keen baker they can be packaged into pretty screw-top glass jars to be used in baking.

Using a small, sharp knife, cut through the skins of the oranges, through the peel and pith and just down to the fruit, dividing the oranges into quarter segments. Carefully remove the peel still in the quarters, trying to leave as much of the pith attached to the skin as possible. Repeat with the grapefruit and lemon. Slice each piece of peel into strips no wider than 2in (1cm). Discard the fruit.

Place the strips in a large saucepan, cover with cold water, and bring to a boil. Simmer for 2–3 minutes, then drain through a colander. Repeat this blanching twice more, using fresh water each time. This will remove any bitterness from the peel.

Wash and dry the saucepan. Place the sugar and 2 cups water in the rinsed-out saucepan. Split the vanilla bean in half down its length, and add to the saucepan with the black peppercorns and cardamom pods. Bring slowly to a boil, stirring from time to time to dissolve the sugar. Add the blanched citrus peels and reduce the heat to a very gentle simmer. Continue to cook for around 2–3 hours, until the peels are very tender and become translucent. This time will vary depending on the variety of fruit used and how thickly you have cut the peels.

Using tongs, remove the peels from the syrup, draining off any excess, and put them on a large sheet of nonstick parchment paper in a single layer. Leave the candied peels to dry and for the sugar to crystallize—this can take anything up to 2–3 days, but will depend on the temperature of your kitchen.

The candied peels can be left as they are but are all the more delicious when half coated in melted dark chocolate.

 Toss the candied peels in superfine sugar before packaging. In an airtight box or jar, they will keep for up to 1 month.

MAKES ENOUGH FOR 2–3 GIFTS

2 oranges
1 pink grapefruit
1 lemon
2¼ cups superfine sugar
1 vanilla bean
½ teaspoon black peppercorns, lightly crushed
4 cardamom pods, lightly crushed
melted dark chocolate to coat (optional)

Vin d'Oranges

MAKES 2 X 17floz (500ml)
WINE BOTTLES

3 cups fruity rosé wine

⅓ cup and 2 tablespoons vodka

⅓ cup and 2 tablespoons brandy

1 vanilla bean

1 large or 2 small cinnamon sticks

scant cup superfine sugar

3 large Seville oranges

1 lemon

This recipe uses Seville oranges, which are only in season for a short time and are more commonly used to make marmalade. If you can't find Seville or bitter oranges for this recipe you could use ordinary oranges and perhaps slightly less sugar. Decant the Vin d'Oranges into pretty bottles and serve chilled.

Pour the wine, vodka, and brandy into a large (just over 3 quarts/ 3 liters), sterilized mason jar (see page 168). Split the vanilla bean in half and add to the jar with the cinnamon and sugar. Seal the jar securely and give it a good shake to dissolve the sugar into the alcohol.

Wash the oranges and the lemon and pat dry on paper towels. Cut the fruit in half and then into ¼in. (5mm) thick slices. Add the sliced oranges and lemon to the jar, seal, and shake again.

Leave the vin d'oranges in the refrigerator for about 1 month, giving it a good shake every now and then. Strain, decant into pretty sterilized bottles (see page 168), and label.

 It will keep, decanted, in the refrigerator, for 2–3 months.

Rhubarb and Vanilla Vodka

MAKES 1 LARGE BOTTLE

1¼lb rhubarb, trimmed weight

1 vanilla bean

1⅛ cups superfine sugar

1 x 25fl oz (750ml) bottle of good-quality vodka

I can highly recommend serving this vodka ice-cold as a martini—though don't be fooled by it's innocent-looking and sweet-tasting pinkness...

For this recipe you really must use the forced Barbie-pink rhubarb as this is what gives the finished vodka its delicate blush color.

Rinse the rhubarb under cold running water, cut into ¾in. (2cm) lengths and place in a shallow saucepan. Split the vanilla bean in half down its length. Using the point of a sharp knife, scrape the seeds out of each half and add the seeds and bean to the saucepan along with the superfine sugar.

Stir over low heat until the sugar has dissolved, then continue to cook for about 3–5 minutes, until the rhubarb is just starting to soften and release its beautiful pink juice. Remove the saucepan from the heat and let cool.

Spoon the contents of the saucepan into a sterilized just over 4-pint (2 liter) mason jar (see page 168). Pour over the vodka, stir well, and seal the jar securely. Leave in the refrigerator for about 2 months, shaking the jar once a week, until the vodka is pink and scented with the rhubarb and vanilla. Strain through cheesecloth and decant into pretty bottles.

 It will keep for up to 3 months in the refrigerator.

SUMMER

CHAPTER 2

Apple and Mint Jelly

How wonderful would it be if you were able to use homegrown apples and garden mint for this scrumptious jelly? I find jellies easier to make in smaller batches and so have suggested bottling this in little jars, and besides it's too special for every day. Perfect with roast lamb.

Wash the apples and cut out any large bruises. Quarter the unpeeled apples and cut into chunks, but do not remove the cores and seeds. Put them into a preserving saucepan or large saucepan, add 2½ cups water, cover the saucepan, and cook gently until the apple chunks have fallen apart and are very soft.

Transfer the contents of the saucepan into a jelly bag, suspend over a large bowl and leave the juice to slowly drip through. This will take at least 4 hours. Do not be tempted to push or prod the apples or the resulting juice will be cloudy.

Pour the juice into a measuring cup and make a note of the amount. For every 2½ cups of juice you will need 2¼ cups of granulated sugar. Pour the juice back into a clean saucepan, then add the sugar and heat gently until it has dissolved. Bring to a boil and cook for a couple of minutes, then add the vinegar and salt. Continue to cook at a steady boil until setting point has been reached (see page 168) for about 10 minutes, removing any scum from the surface with a large spoon.

Remove the saucepan from the heat and let cool for 5 minutes. Add the chopped mint and stir to distribute it evenly throughout the jelly. Pour the jelly into small, sterilized jars (see page 168) and seal immediately.

Label the jars once completely cold. Jelly will keep for months if stored unopened in a cool, dark cupboard or cellar. Once opened, store in the refrigerator and use within 1 month.

MAKES 4 SMALL JARS

2¼lb (1kg) apples (variety suitable for cooking)

approx. 2¼ cups granulated sugar

4 tablespoons white wine vinegar

½ teaspoon salt

4–5 tablespoons finely chopped fresh mint

Strawberry and Rose Petal Cordial

If you're lucky (and green thumbed) enough to grow old-fashioned scented roses, then spare a handful or two of the petals to be added to this cordial. Store the cordial in the refrigerator and serve diluted to taste with sparkling water or club soda and plenty of ice.
Or pour a generous glug over vanilla ice cream and add a handful of sliced summer berries for a scrumptious ice cream sundae.

Put the sugar into a medium-size saucepan and add 1¼ cups of cold water. Using a vegetable peeler, pare the zest from the lemon in strips and add to the saucepan along with the squeezed lemon juice. Set the saucepan over low to medium heat, stirring occasionally to dissolve the sugar, then bring to a boil and simmer for 2 minutes.

Remove the saucepan from the heat and add the strawberries, rose petals, and citric acid. Gently crush the berries in the saucepan with the back of a spoon. Leave the fruit and petals to steep in the syrup for about 4 hours.

Strain the cordial through a fine sieve or cheesecloth, then pour into sterilized bottles (see page 168), seal and label. Store in the refrigerator until ready to serve.

 It will keep, in the refrigerator, for a couple of weeks.

MAKES ABOUT 2 cups

1⅓ cups superfine sugar

juice and zest of 1 organic lemon

18oz (500g) ripe hulled strawberries, quartered

2 handfuls of fragrant, unsprayed rose petals, washed

1 teaspoon citric acid

Summer Berry Vodka

Serve this berry-infused vodka in cocktails or ice cold in little shot glasses. You could also try adding a dash to Champagne as an alternative Kir Royale.

Place the raspberries, strawberries, lemon zest, and superfine sugar in a large bowl and lightly crush with the back of a wooden spoon or fork. Add the vanilla bean, mix well, and leave to one side for about 2 hours, until the sugar has dissolved and the fruit starts to become really juicy.

Spoon the contents of the bowl into a large sterilized mason jar (see page 168) and pour in the vodka. Mix well and chill for 1 week or until needed (up to about a month).

Strain the vodka through a fine sieve or cheesecloth, and decant into pretty sterilized bottles.

 It will keep, in the refrigerator, for up to 2 months.

MAKES ABOUT 3¼ cups

¾ cup raspberries

¾ cup strawberries, hulled and quartered

pared zest of 1 organic lemon

scant cup superfine sugar

1 vanilla bean, halved

1 x 25fl oz (750ml) bottle of good-quality vodka

There's nothing quite like homemade lemon curd. And when you add passion fruit to the mix, you're on to something really special. Serve it with freshly baked scones (or shortcakes), hot buttered English muffins, or spread between vanilla cake layers with lashings of whipped cream and fresh berries.

Lemon and Passion Fruit Curd

Beat the eggs and strain into a medium-size heatproof bowl. Add the remaining ingredients and place the bowl over a saucepan of simmering water. Do not allow the bottom of the bowl to come into contact with the water or the heat will scramble the eggs.

Stir the mixture constantly until it reaches the consistency of very thick custard. Remove from the heat and stand the bowl in a sink of cold water to speed up the cooling process, stirring occasionally until cold.

Pour into sterilized jars (see page 168), cover, and store in the refrigerator until needed.

It will keep, in the refrigerator, for up to 1 week.

MAKES 4 SMALL JARS

4 large eggs

1 ⅛ sticks unsalted butter, cubed

1 cup superfine sugar

zest and juice of 3 organic lemons

seeds and pulp of 2 passion fruit

Hot Chili Pepper Jelly

I would suggest making this fiery little number in small batches—not only does a little go a long way, but it's a true labor of love chopping those chili peppers.

MAKES 3–4 SMALL JARS

1lb 10oz (750g) Macintosh apples

approx. 1⅛ cups granulated sugar

½ teaspoon salt

2 tablespoons white wine vinegar

4–5 red chili peppers, seeded

1 red bell pepper, seeded

Wash the apples and cut into chunks (peel, core, and seeds included). Place the apple chunks into a saucepan, add 1¾ cups and 2 table-spoons water, cover, and cook over a low to medium heat until the apples are really tender and have fallen apart. Scoop the contents of the saucepan into a jelly bag suspended over a bowl, and leave for at least 4 hours or overnight to allow the apple juice to slowly drip through. Do not be tempted to push the apples through the bag or the resulting jelly will be cloudy.

The next day, pour the strained juice into a measuring cup and make a note of the quantity. Pour the juice back into a clean saucepan and add 2¼ cups of granulated sugar per 2½ cups of apple juice. Put the saucepan over low heat and stir to dissolve the sugar, then bring to a boil. Simmer for a couple of minutes, then add the salt and vinegar.

Continue to cook at a steady boil until setting point is reached (see page 168), which will most likely take about 10 minutes.

While the jelly is boiling, prepare the chili peppers and red bell pepper. Roughly chop them and blend quickly in a food processor until finely chopped. Once the jelly reaches setting point, add the chopped chili peppers and bell pepper to the saucepan and continue to cook for a further 2 minutes.

Take the saucepan off the heat and let the jelly settle for 2 minutes before pouring into small, sterilized jars (see page 168). Seal immediately and let cool completely before labeling.

This jelly can be used immediately as it's not like a chutney where the vinegar and spices need to mellow. Store in a cool, dark cupboard or cellar. Once opened, store in the refrigerator and use within 1 month.

Red Currant Curd

Look out for little punnets of jewel-like red currants in the fruit and vegetable stores during the summer months and try this as an alternative to lemon curd.

Strip the red currants from their stalks, using a fork. Place in a small saucepan with a splash of water and cook over low heat for about 5 minutes, until the currants are very soft. Push the fruit and juice through a nylon sieve into a bowl.

Return the red currant purée to a clean saucepan and add the superfine sugar (varying the amount depending on how sweet the purée is) and the butter. Stir over low heat until the butter has melted and the sugar has dissolved.

Beat the whole egg and yolks together in a small bowl, then whisk in 2–3 tablespoons of the hot red currant mixture. Return the whole mixture to the saucepan. Stirring constantly, cook over low heat for about 2 minutes, until thickened. Do not allow the curd to boil or the eggs will scramble.

Strain the curd into a pitcher, then pour into dry sterilized jars (see page 168) and seal.

Keep in the refrigerator and use within 1 week. Attach a label to the jar with serving suggestions such as spooning the curd in between buttery layers of vanilla-scented cake and lightly whipped heavy cream or spreading into miniature sweet pie shells and topping with a pillow of meringue.

MAKES 2 JARS

2⅔ cups red currants

scant–generous ½ cup superfine sugar

¼ stick unsalted butter

1 large egg

2 large egg yolks

Strawberry and Vanilla Preserves

A recipe for the height of summer when soft fruit is at its best, perfectly ripe, and intensely sweet. Preserves have a slightly softer set than jam as the fruit remains whole or in large pieces and for this reason it really is important to use small, ripe strawberries. The result will be a pot of the most intense strawberry flavor with a vibrant red color. The hint of vanilla seeds will enhance the strawberry flavor without overpowering it. I'm thinking scones, clotted cream, and lazy, sunny afternoons in the garden...

Pour the sugar into a preserving saucepan or other large saucepan. Add the lemon juice and 2 tablespoons of water. Split the vanilla bean in half lengthwise, then using the tip of a small knife scrape out the little black seeds and add the bean and seeds to the saucepan. Set over low heat and stir from time to time until the sugar has dissolved.

Remove the saucepan from the heat, add the strawberries, and stir gently to coat in the hot syrup. Let stand for 30–60 minutes, to allow the fruit to soften and release its juice into the syrup.

Return the saucepan to medium heat and cook at a steady boil, without stirring, for about 10 minutes, or until the preserve reaches setting point (see page 168).

Remove the saucepan from the heat, discard the vanilla bean and let the preserve cool in the saucepan for about 10 minutes as this ensures that the strawberries are evenly distributed throughout once the preserve is bottled.

Carefully spoon into sterilized jars (see page 168) and seal immediately. Let cool completely before labelling.

 This will keep for months, unopened, in a cool, dark cupboard or cellar and, once opened, for up to 1 month in the refrigerator.

MAKES 3–4 SMALL JARS
2¼ cups granulated sugar
juice of 1 lemon
1 vanilla bean
1lb 3oz (550g) small ripe strawberries, hulled

Cherry Jam

MAKES 3 X 1lb (450g) JARS

1lb 10oz ripe cherries

3 cups granulated sugar

liquid or powdered pectin (optional): use according to package instructions if set is not achieved

juice of ½ a lemon

This is one of my favorite homemade jams. The cherries are pitted and kept whole which make the jam somehow more indulgent, especially when spooned onto toasted buttered biscuits or homemade English muffins.

Remove the pits from the cherries, using a cherry pitter if you have one. Place the cherries in a large, solid-based saucepan or preserving saucepan and add 3–4 tablespoons water. Set the saucepan over low to medium heat and cook gently until the cherries are very soft.

Add the sugar and lemon juice and stir gently until the sugar has dissolved. Increase the heat slightly and boil steadily for 20 minutes, or until setting point has been reached (see page 168).

Remove the saucepan from the heat and let the jam rest for 10–15 minutes before spooning into sterilized jars (see page 168). Resting the jam will cool it sufficiently so that the cherries are suspended rather than sinking to the bottom of the jars. Cover immediately and let the jam cool completely before labelling.

 This will keep for months, unopened, in a cool, dark cupboard or cellar and, once opened, for up to 1 month in the refrigerator.

Seedless Black Currant Jam

MAKES 2 X 1lb (450g) JARS

4½ cups blackcurrants

2¼ cups granulated sugar

liquid or powdered pectin (optional): use according to package instructions if set is not achieved

Although this doesn't make a vast quantity of jam, the end result is so intense that a small teaspoonful will instantly transport you to high summer. Sublime on hot buttered toast!

Place the black currants in a large saucepan with 1 cup water. Bring slowly to a boil, then reduce the heat, and simmer gently for about 3 minutes, to allow the fruit to soften and burst.

Press the fruit and juice though a nylon sieve set over a bowl to extract all the pulp and remove the seeds.

Return the black currant pulp to the clean saucepan and add the sugar. Stir constantly over low heat until the sugar has dissolved, then increase the heat, and boil rapidly until setting point has been reached (see page 168)—this will take no more than 10 minutes.

Pour the jam into sterilized jars (see page 168) and seal immediately.

 This will keep for months, unopened, in a cool, dark cupboard or cellar and, once opened, for up to 1 month in the refrigerator.

Raspberry and Passion Fruit Pastilles

Cut these pastilles into small squares, toss in superfine sugar and pack into pretty glass candy jars tied with ribbons and a gift tag. One batch of this recipe will make enough pastilles to fill a couple of jars making two gifts at once.

Try using a small heart-shaped cutter to stamp out the pastilles, toss in sugar, and package into little bags or boxes as wedding favors or Valentines gifts. Any trimmings are a little gift to yourself.

Lightly oil a 6¾in. (17cm) square baking pan and line with nonstick parchment paper.

Place the raspberries into a solid-bottomed shallow saucepan. Halve the passion fruit and scoop the seeds and juice into the saucepan. Add the lemon juice, cover the saucepan, and cook over medium heat until the raspberries have softened and cooked down to a pulp.

Remove from the heat and push the fruit through a fine nylon sieve into a bowl. Weigh the resulting purée and return it to a clean saucepan. Add an equal quantity of sugar and stir over a low to medium heat until it has dissolved. Continue to cook for about 30 minutes, stirring frequently with a wooden spoon, until the purée has reduced and thickened considerably to the consistency of jam and reached setting point (see page 168).

Use a silicone spatula to scoop the purée into the prepared pan and let set for at least 6 hours or overnight.

Cover a baking sheet with a sheet of nonstick parchment paper sprinkled liberally with superfine sugar. Flip the pastille mixture out of the pan and on to the sugar-covered paper, and carefully peel off the backing paper. Cut into pastilles and toss in the superfine sugar to coat completely. Let dry for 1 hour before packaging.

 Store in an airtight jar. These pastilles will keep for 4–5 days.

MAKES 20 PIECES

14oz (400g) raspberries
3 passion fruit
juice of ¼ lemon
1½ cups granulated sugar, or more
liquid or powdered pectin (optional): use according to package instructions if set is not achieved
superfine sugar, to serve

Love Heart Sugar Cubes

Not really cubes at all. These little sugar hearts would make the perfect gift for valentines, a bridal shower or as a wedding favor. You could tint the sugar almost any color imaginable but pale, pastel shades are more elegant when teamed with vintage tea cups. Why stop at love heart sugar cubes?

Look out for small star or simple flower shaped cutters to experiment with.

MAKES LOTS!

1⅛ cups superfine sugar
food coloring pastes
(pink and other
pastel colors)

Line 2 baking sheets with nonstick parchment paper. Put the sugar into a bowl, add 1–2 tablespoons cold water, and stir thoroughly until the sugar takes on the texture of damp sand, the kind you'd use to make sandcastles, adding more water or sugar to achieve the correct texture.

Pour half the mixture on to one of the baking sheets and press firmly to a thickness of ½in. (1cm). Using a small heart-shaped cookie cutter, stamp out shapes, one at a time. Using your fingers, gently push each sugar heart out of the cutter and on to the second baking sheet. Repeat until you have used up all the white sugar mixture.

Using a toothpick, add a tiny amount of pink food coloring paste to the remaining mixture and stir until combined. Stamp out more hearts in the same way. Let dry overnight.

Package into pretty boxes. They will keep for up to 1 month.

Cherry Tomato and Sweet Chili Pepper Jam

A number of recipes in this book would be perfect to make and give together—this is one such recipe. I can't get enough of this sweet, spicy relish spread on top of Oatmeal Crackers for Cheese (page 120) with some tangy marinated goat cheese (page 58) crumbled on top.

MAKES 3–4 X 9oz (250g) JARS

2 onions

1lb 10oz (750g) ripe cherry tomatoes, halved

2 fat garlic cloves, minced

2 large mild red chili peppers, seeded and finely chopped

2in. (5cm) piece of fresh ginger, grated

2 teaspoons cumin seeds

2 teaspoons coriander seeds

1 cup white wine vinegar

1½ cups soft light brown sugar

2 teaspoons fish sauce (or soy sauce if making this for vegetarians)

Peel and finely chop the onions and place in a wide saucepan with the tomatoes, garlic, chili peppers, and ginger.

Toast the cumin and coriander seeds in a small, dry skillet over low heat for 1 minute until aromatic, then remove from the skillet and grind in a mortar and pestle. Add to the saucepan along with the wine vinegar and sugar.

Cook over low to medium heat until the sugar has dissolved. Bring to a boil, then reduce the heat to a simmer and continue to cook until the mixture has reduced to a syrupy jam consistency, stirring from time to time. Add the fish sauce (or soy sauce) and cook for a further couple of minutes before spooning into small sterilized jars (see page 168). Seal the jars while hot and let cool completely before labeling and storing.

 This will keep for months, unopened, in a cool, dark cupboard or cellar and, once opened, for up to 1 month in the refrigerator.

Spice Mix

With a jar of this spice mix, a couple of fabulous steaks, some spiced plum Barbecue Sauce (page 56), and a bottle of Chili Pepper Vodka (page 167), you could find yourself the number one guest at any summer barbecue.

Lightly bruise and crack the cardamom pods using a mortar and pestle or by giving them a sharp tap with a rolling pin. Remove and discard the papery green outer husks and put the little black seeds into a dry skillet. Add the peppercorns and the cumin, coriander and fennel seeds. Toast the spices in a dry skillet over low heat for about 2–3 minutes, until they start to smell very aromatic and begin to brown slightly.

Immediately put the toasted seeds into the mortar, add the crushed red pepper flakes, and finely grind with the pestle. Add the remaining ingredients to the mortar and mix to combine.

Scoop the spice mix into a sterilized jar (see page 168), seal, and label with grilling instructions.

Sprinkle spice mix over steaks, chicken or veggies and leave to marinade before grilling. Stored in a screwtop jar, it will keep for up to 1 month.

MAKES 1 X REGULAR JAM JAR

6 cardamom pods

2 teaspoons black peppercorns

4 teaspoons cumin seeds

4 teaspoons coriander seeds

4 teaspoons fennel seeds

1 teaspoon crushed red pepper flakes

2 teaspoons dried oregano

1 teaspoon paprika

2 teaspoons sea salt

1 rounded teaspoon dry mustard powder

3–4 teaspoons superfine sugar

Spiced Plum Sauce for Grilling

Not only would this sauce be the thing to serve alongside chargrilled sausages and burgers but it's not half-bad when basted over grilled ribs and chicken.

Wash the plums, cut them into quarters, and remove the pits. Peel and chop the onions and put into a preserving saucepan or large saucepan with the plums. Add the garlic and ginger and put all the spices in a cheesecloth bag and also add to the saucepan.

Add the sugar and vinegar and set the saucepan over medium heat, stirring from time to time until the sugar has dissolved. Bring the mixture slowly to a boil, then reduce to a gentle simmer and continue to cook until the plums and onions are very soft. This can take about 1 hour.

Remove the cheesecloth bag of spices and pour the sauce into a food mill set over a clean saucepan. Stir it through a food mill to remove any tough plum skins. Place the saucepan over low to medium heat and continue to cook for about 10 minutes, until thickened to the consistency of tomato ketchup.

Taste, and add the soy sauce and a little more sugar if needed to balance the flavors.

Carefully pour the sauce into sterilized jars or bottles (see page 168) and seal. Let cool before labeling.

 Store for months unopened in a cool, dark cupboard or cellar. Once opened, store in the refrigerator and use within 1 month.

MAKES 4 X 1lb (450g) JARS

3lb 5oz (1.5kg) red or purple plums

2 small onions

2 fat garlic cloves, peeled and sliced

2in. (5cm) piece of fresh ginger, grated

1 teaspoon black peppercorns

1 small cinnamon stick

4 allspice berries

2 teaspoons sea salt

2 star anise

5 whole cloves

1½ cups soft light brown sugar

2 cups white wine vinegar

1–2 tablespoons soy sauce

Scandinavian-Style Crispbread

I like to use a combination of flours for these crispbreads—rye, wholewheat, spelt, and maybe even some white bread flour all work well. Traditionally the crispbreads would be rolled with a special knobbly rolling pin before baking, but pricking them all over with a fork or pressing the fine side of a grater over the surface of each one works just as well.

MAKES 3 OR 4 X 9oz (250g) JARS

1 teaspoon active dry yeast

1 teaspoon honey

scant 5 cups rye flour or a combination of flours (see above), plus extra for rolling out

1 teaspoon sea salt flakes, plus a little extra

1 teaspoon caraway seeds, lightly crushed

1 teaspoon poppy seeds

1 teaspoon sesame seeds

Whisk the yeast and honey into approximately 1¼ cups warm water in a pitcher and leave in a warm place for around 5 minutes until a light, yeasty foam forms on top of the water.

Pour the flour into a large bowl, stir in the salt, caraway, poppy, and sesame seeds and make a well in the middle of the dry ingredients. Pour the yeasty water into the bowl and mix with a wooden spoon until the mixture comes together into a ball. Turn out onto a clean countertop and knead lightly for about 3–4 minutes until smooth. Shape into a ball, return the dough to the bowl, cover with plastic wrap and leave to rise in a warm place for 1 hour.

Preheat the oven to 375°F (190°C).

Lightly dust the countertop with flour and divide the dough into 12–16 even-size balls. Roll each piece out as thinly as possible and, using a bread-and-butter plate as a guide, cut each piece into a neat disk. Using a 1½in. (4cm) round cutter, stamp out a small disk from the middle of each piece, prick the dough with a fork or press the surface with a grater, scatter with a little more sea salt, and bake in batches on the middle rack of the preheated oven for around 10 minutes until crisp and golden, turning the crispbreads over halfway through the baking time.

Cool completely before packaging and tie a ribbon through the hole.

These crispbreads would be delicious with gravad lax (page 164) or pork rillettes (page 64), or simply served with soft herby cheese. Stored in an airtight box, they will keep for a couple of weeks.

Marinated Goat Cheese

I prefer the small young Crottin goat cheeses for this recipe and some fine quality, fruity olive oil for the marinade to make this really special. I have suggested using fresh oregano but you could just as easily use a couple of sprigs of rosemary or thyme. A jar of these cheeses would make a tasty addition to any picnic basket or summer cheese board.

Pack the cheeses into a sterilized, wide-necked storage jar (see page 168), and add the bay leaf and oregano leaves. Cut the chili pepper in half through the stalk and pare 2 strips of zest from the lemon. Arrange the chili pepper and lemon zest around the cheeses. Add the fennel seeds and garlic cloves, and pour over extra virgin olive oil so that the cheeses are completely covered. Seal the jar and chill. Bring back to room temperature to serve.

Store in the refrigerator for up to 1 week until needed and then drain and eat with some fabulous bread, crumbled into salads or broiled on slices of baguette with a good spoonful of Tomato Chutney (page 85).

MAKES 1 LARGE JAR

4 young Crottin goat cheeses
1 bay leaf
½ tablespoon fresh oregano leaves
1 red bird's-eye chili pepper
1 organic lemon
½ teaspoon fennel seeds
2 garlic cloves, peeled and halved
extra virgin olive oil, to cover

Pesto

Everyone is familiar with this classic Italian basil sauce. Pesto couldn't be easier to make and when it's homemade it's a thing of beauty—a stunning vibrant green color with a taste of pure summer. Give a little jar of this sauce that's loaded with fresh basil, pine nuts, and Pecorino Romano with a box of fresh tortellini (page 88) and snappy grissini sticks (page 87).

MAKES 2 SMALL JARS

3⅛ cups basil leaves

2–3 fat garlic cloves, roughly chopped

½ cup pine nuts

1 cup fruity olive oil, plus more

⅔ cup finely grated Pecorino Romano cheese

salt and freshly ground black pepper

Put the basil, garlic, and pine nuts into the bowl of a food processor. Blend the ingredients until they are roughly chopped, then add almost all the olive oil and blend again until finely chopped and combined. Mix in the grated Pecorino Romano, taste and add salt and freshly ground black pepper.

Spoon the pesto into small sterilized jars (see page 168). Pour a little olive oil over the top and seal. Label and store in the refrigerator until you are ready to give it as a present.

 Pesto will keep, in the refrigerator, for up to 1 week.

Pickled Vegetables
for Pâté and Picnics

An absolute must for serving alongside Pork Rillettes (page 64)
or any pâté or terrine which might need something sharp and crunchy
to cut through the richness.

Prepare the vegetables the day before you want to bottle the pickles, as
they need to brine overnight in the salt.

Top and tail the zucchini, cut in half lengthwise and cut into ½in. (1cm)
thick slices or dice. Seed the bell pepper and cut into ½in. (1cm) thick
chunks or strips. Top and tail the French beans and cut into ¾in. (2cm)
lengths. Peel the carrot and cut into pieces the same size as the zucchini.
Peel the onions and cut into small wedges through the root. Put all the
vegetables into a plastic or ceramic bowl, toss with the sea salt, cover,
and leave overnight.

The next day, rinse the vegetables under cold running water and pat dry
on paper towels.

Put the vinegar into a saucepan with the spices, bay leaf, and garlic. Bring
to a boil, then reduce the heat, and simmer very gently for 5 minutes so
that the spices can infuse into the vinegar.

Spoon the vegetables into a sterilized jar (see page 168), add the
tarragon, and pour over the hot vinegar, ensuring that all of the
vegetables are completely covered. Seal the jar immediately and let cool
completely before labeling. Store for 1 month before opening.

 Store for months unopened in a cool, dark cupboard or cellar.
Once opened, store in the refrigerator and use within 2 months.

MAKES 1 LARGE JAR

1 zucchini

1 red bell pepper

1 handful of French beans

1 medium carrot

2 small onions

1 tablespoon sea salt

¾ cup white wine vinegar

**1 teaspoon yellow mustard
seeds**

½ teaspoon black peppercorns

4 allspice berries

½ teaspoon coriander seeds

1 bay leaf

**2 garlic cloves, peeled and
halved**

2 sprigs of fresh tarragon

Ginger and Lemongrass Cooler

Serve this refreshing summer cordial diluted to taste with club soda or sparkling water and plenty of ice as a twist on ginger beer.

Place the sugar, lemon zest, and juice with 4 cups of water in a large saucepan. Cut the lemongrass stalks in half, give them a good bash with a rolling pin to bruise the stems and add to the saucepan.

Whiz the peeled ginger in a food processor until finely chopped. Add to the saucepan and bring the mixture slowly to a boil. Reduce to a very gentle simmer and continue to cook for another 20 minutes. Remove the saucepan from the heat and leave the syrup to one side for about 4 hours, to allow the ginger and lemongrass to impart maximum flavor.

Bring the syrup to a boil again, add the citric acid, and stir to dissolve. Strain the syrup through a fine sieve or a piece of cheesecloth, then pour into sterilized bottles (see page 168), using a funnel, and seal. Label the bottles when cold.

Serve diluted to taste with club soda or sparkling water and plenty of ice. It will keep in the refrigerator for up to 1 month.

MAKES ABOUT 4 cups

2¼ cups superfine sugar

pared zest and juice of 1 organic lemon

3 sticks of lemongrass

4½oz (125g) peeled fresh ginger

1 teaspoon citric acid

Pork Rillettes

Rillettes are a type of rustic pâté where pork belly is cooked very slowly with plenty of seasoning and herbs until meltingly tender, it's then shredded before being packed into jars and sealed with a layer of fat. Spoon rillettes onto rustic bread and serve with Pickled Vegetables (page 62).

Preheat the oven to 300°F (150°C). Cut the pork belly into ¾in. (2cm) pieces and place in a large bowl. Dice the bacon and add to the bowl.

Lightly crush the juniper berries and peppercorns in a mortar and pestle and add to the bowl along with the mace, garlic, thyme, and bay leaf. Season well with sea salt and black pepper.

Pour over the white wine, mix well, then transfer to a large solid casserole or terrine dish and cover with a tight-fitting lid. Cook on the bottom rack of the preheated oven for 3–3½ hours, or until the pork is completely tender and falling apart, and stirring once or twice during the cooking time.

Remove from the oven and pour the meat into a colander set over a bowl. Discard the thyme, bay leaf, peppercorns, and juniper berries. Put the drained meat into another bowl, then pull it into shreds, using 2 forks. Taste for seasoning, adding more salt and pepper if needed. Pack the meat into sterilized jars (see page 168), or a terrine or earthenware dish, and pour over a little of the liquid that drained into the bowl.

When the meat is cool, cover and chill for 30 minutes. Pour over a layer of the strained fat or goose fat, seal the jars, and chill until ready to serve.

Stored in the refrigerator, rillettes will keep for a couple of weeks provided the meat is covered with a good layer of fat. Bring back to room temperature to serve.

MAKES 3 X 1lb (450g) JARS

3lb 5oz (1.5kg) boned and skinned pork belly

4 slices smoked bacon

6 juniper berries

6 black peppercorns

1 blade of mace

5 fat garlic cloves, peeled and sliced

2 large sprigs of fresh thyme

1 bay leaf

sea salt and freshly ground black pepper

1¼ cups dry white wine

2–4 tablespoons goose fat (optional)

FALL

CHAPTER 3

Apricot and Almond Brownies

These brownies are definitely for grown-ups—they are rich, dense, and deeply fudgy. Give them as a thank-you gift for dinner in place of a store-bought box of chocolates. Cut into small squares they are delicious with coffee, tea or just about anything.

Preheat the oven to 325°F (170°C). Grease and line the base of a square 9in. (23cm) baking pan with nonstick parchment paper.

Warm the Marsala or brandy in a small saucepan, add the chopped apricots, and let soak for 10 minutes.

Toast the almonds for 5 minutes on a baking sheet in the preheated oven, then let cool and roughly chop.

Melt the butter and chocolate together either in a bowl set over a saucepan of barely simmering water or in the microwave on a low setting. Stir until smooth and let cool slightly.

Whisk the eggs and sugar in a bowl, add the vanilla, and whisk into the melted chocolate. Sift the flour and fold into the mixture along with the chopped almonds and soaked apricots. Pour into the prepared pan and bake on the middle rack of the oven for 25 minutes until the top has formed a crust but the underneath is still soft. Cool in the pan, then cut into squares.

 Stored in an airtight container, they will keep for 2–3 days.

MAKES ABOUT 16 BROWNIES

2–3 tablespoons Marsala or brandy

scant 1 cup dried apricots, roughly chopped

1 cup blanched almonds

1⅓ sticks unsalted butter, diced

8oz (225g) dark chocolate (72% cacao), chopped

4 large eggs

1½ cups soft light brown or light muscovado sugar

1 teaspoon vanilla extract

1 cup all-purpose flour

Honeycomb

Honeycomb and chocolate—the perfect combination for Halloween or camping trips.

Line a 8in. square baking pan with lightly oiled foil. Half fill the sink with cold water and have ready a whisk and the baking soda.

Place the sugar, syrup, cream of tartar, and vinegar into a medium-size, solid-based saucepan. Add 5 tablespoons water and set the saucepan over medium heat. Stir until the sugar has dissolved, then bring the mixture to a boil. Continue to cook until the mixture turns amber-colored and reaches "hard crack" stage, or 300°F (154°C) on a candy thermometer.

As soon as the caramel reaches the right temperature, remove the saucepan from the heat and plunge into the sink of cold water to speed up the cooling process. Working quickly, pour the baking soda into the caramel and whisk to combine evenly; the mixture will foam up like a mini volcano. Pour into the prepared pan in an even layer and let cool.

Melt the chocolate in a bowl set over a saucepan of barely simmering water and stir until smooth. Remove from the heat and cool slightly. Turn the honeycomb out of the pan, peel off the foil, and break into chunks. Half dip each piece into the melted chocolate. Let harden before packaging.

 Stored in an airtight container, it will keep for 2–3 days.

MAKES ABOUT 20 PIECES

1⅓ cups superfine sugar
½ cup corn syrup
pinch of cream of tartar
1 teaspoon white wine vinegar
1½ teaspoons baking soda
5½oz (150g) dark or milk chocolate

Chocolate and Hazelnut Spread

A grown-up version of a childhood favorite, this is delicious when spread thickly onto toast, inbetween cake layers, or when sandwiched in the middle of cookies—or if no-one's looking straight from the jar with a big spoon...

Preheat the oven to 350°F (180°C). Turn the hazelnuts out onto a baking sheet and toast in the preheated oven for about 5–7 minutes, until pale golden. Remove the nuts from the oven and cool slightly. Put the warm hazelnuts into a food processor and chop until they become an almost smooth paste.

Gently melt the chocolate, condensed milk, and hazelnut oil in a small saucepan over low heat. Stir until smooth and add to the hazelnut paste in the food processor. Add a pinch of salt and blend, then add the hot water and blend again until the mixture has a thick, spreadable consistency.

Spoon into a pretty sterilized jar (see page 168) and let cool. Cover with a lid and label when cold.

 It will keep in the refrigerator for up to 2 weeks.

MAKES 1 X 1lb (450g) JAR

½ cup blanched hazelnuts

3½oz (100g) dark chocolate (72% cacao), chopped

⅓ cup and 2 tablespoons sweetened condensed milk

1–2 tablespoons hazelnut oil

pinch of salt

3–4 tablespoons hot water

English Muffins

Muffins make an irresistible afternoon tea when split in half, toasted, and spread with lashings of butter and homemade cherry jam or chocolate spread (see pages 49 and 72). They'd be just perfect after a bracing walk in the fall chill or toasted over an open fire on a Sunday afternoon.

Heat the milk in a large saucepan until it is warm to the touch, then add the sugar and yeast and stir well. Leave to one side for about 5 minutes, until the yeast has formed a thick, foamy crust on top of the milk.

Put the flour and salt into the bowl of a stand mixer fitted with a dough hook. Pour the milk mixture into the flour and knead on medium speed for about 5–7 minutes, until the dough is silky and smooth but not wet.

Turn the dough out on to a work surface lightly dusted with flour and knead briefly by hand to bring it into a neat ball. Place in a large, clean bowl, cover with plastic wrap and leave in a warm, draft-free place for around 1 hour, or until the dough has doubled in size.

Lightly dust the work surface and a large baking sheet with a little more flour. Turn the dough on to the work surface and knead again for 1 minute, then roll out to a thickness of just over ½ in. (1cm). Using a plain round 2¾–3in. (7–8cm) cutter, stamp out muffins from the dough and place well apart on the floured baking sheet. Re-roll the dough scraps and stamp out more muffins. You should end up with about 8–10 muffins in total.

Cover loosely with oiled plastic wrap, and set aside for another 30–40 minutes to rise again until doubled in height.

Heat a griddle saucepan or solid-based skillet over medium heat and cook the muffins in batches over low heat for 5–7 minutes on each side, until well risen and golden brown.

 They will keep for 2–3 days if well wrapped in foil. I would package them wrapped in a pretty cloth or in a basket.

MAKES 8–10 MUFFINS

1⅓ cups milk

2 teaspoons superfine sugar

1½ teaspoons active dry yeast

3¾ cups bread flour, plus extra for dusting

1 teaspoon sea salt

Anzac Cookies

MAKES ABOUT 20 COOKIES

1 cup all-purpose flour
scant cup shredded coconut
1 cup rolled oats
⅓ cup light brown sugar
pinch of salt
1⅛ sticks unsalted butter
2 tablespoons corn syrup
½ teaspoon baking soda
2 tablespoons boiling water

These cookies are a favorite in Australia and New Zealand, where one theory has it that they were baked by the wives and families of soldiers who were fighting in the trenches in World War One. They were packaged into tins and sent by ship to the troops in food parcels. Nowadays they are still popular and a perfect way to enjoy a taste of Australia and New Zealand without getting on a plane.

Preheat the oven to 350°F (180°C) and line 2 baking sheets with nonstick parchment paper.

In a large mixing bowl stir together the flour, coconut, oats, sugar, and salt. Melt the unsalted butter and corn syrup together in a small saucepan set over low heat, or in the microwave on a low to medium setting. Stir until smooth.

In a small bowl mix together the baking soda and boiling water. Add to the dry ingredients along with the melted butter and corn syrup, and stir until smooth.

Roll level tablespoons of the dough into rough balls in your hands and arrange on the prepared baking sheets, leaving plenty of space between them. Flatten them slightly with your hands and bake on the middle rack of the preheated oven for about 15 minutes, until golden brown. Cool the cookies on the trays and package into pretty boxes or bags once completely cold.

These will keep for up to 1 week in an airtight box (although they were originally made to be kept for weeks on long sea journeys to the troops).

Sea-salted Caramels

You really do need a candy thermometer for making caramels and toffees, but it won't be a wasted investment—once you've tried these caramels you'll be hooked. The saltiness is just enough to cut through the intense caramel sweetness, making them dangerously addictive. Wrap each caramel in a twist of nonstick parchment paper.

Grease a 6–6¾ in. (15–17cm) square pan with sunflower oil. Place the superfine sugar in a deep saucepan with 2 tablespoons of cold water. Set the saucepan over medium heat until the sugar has dissolved, then bring to a boil and continue to cook until the sugar has turned to a deep amber-colored caramel. Remove the saucepan from the heat and immediately add the remaining ingredients and stir until smooth.

Return the saucepan to the heat and bring back to a boil. Continue to cook until the caramel reaches 250°F (130°C) on a candy thermometer. Remove from the heat, let settle for 30 seconds, then pour into the prepared pan and leave until cold before turning out of the pan and breaking into pieces.

 These will keep for 4–5 days in an airtight box or wrapped in nonstick parchment paper in a jar.

MAKES ABOUT 20 CARAMELS

sunflower oil, for greasing

⅔ cup superfine sugar

¾ cup light muscovado or light brown sugar

scant ½ cup (⅞ stick) unsalted butter

¾ cup and 2 tablespoons heavy cream

3 tablespoons corn syrup

1 teaspoon sea salt flakes

Peanut or Macadamia Brittle

Use shelled, unsalted macadamia nuts or peanuts for this old-fashioned candy recipe. Break the cooled brittle into chunky pieces and package into bags or boxes lined with waxed paper.

Although delicious eaten just as it is, brittle would be delicious broken into small pieces and scattered over ice cream or a fudgy, frosted chocolate cake.

MAKES ABOUT 20 PIECES

sunflower oil, for greasing
⅓ cup soft light brown sugar
scant cup superfine sugar
¼ cup corn syrup
¼ stick unsalted butter
½ teaspoon baking soda
pinch of salt
1⅛ cups shelled and skinned peanuts or macadamia nuts

Grease a solid baking sheet with sunflower oil.

Pour both sugars and the corn syrup into a medium-size heavy saucepan. Add ⅓ cup water and stir over medium heat until the sugar has completely dissolved. Add the butter and stir until melted.

Bring the mixture to a boil and continue to cook steadily until the temperature reaches 310°F (154°C) on a candy thermometer.

Remove from the heat and immediately add the baking soda, salt, and nuts, stirring well as the mixture foams up. Pour on to the baking sheet and spread level with the back of a wooden spoon.

Once the brittle is completely cold and hardened, break it into pieces and package in cellophane bags.

It will keep for 3–4 days in an airtight box.

Creamy Vanilla Fudge with Chocolate and Nuts

It might be creamy, but this fudge is a little bit richer and more decadent than normal with the addition of dark chocolate and toasted nuts. You could also try adding some rum-soaked raisins or brandy-infused dried morello cherries in place of the nuts.

Line the base and sides of a 6in. (15cm) square baking pan with a sheet of foil lightly greased with sunflower oil.

Place the superfine sugar in a medium-size, solid-based saucepan. Add the evaporated milk, milk, and a pinch of salt and set the saucepan over medium heat to slowly and evenly dissolve the sugar, stirring gently from time to time. Once the sugar has completely dissolved, increase the heat slightly and bring to a gentle boil.

Clamp a candy thermometer on the side of the saucepan, and stirring occasionally to prevent the sugar catching on the bottom of the saucepan, continue to cook the fudge at a gentle boil until it reaches the "soft ball" stage or 240°F (115°C).

Immediately remove the saucepan from the heat and set it on a heatproof surface. Stir in the butter and vanilla extract and let the fudge cool in the saucepan for 2–3 minutes. Once the fudge has cooled slightly, beat it vigorously with a wooden spoon for about 5 minutes until the fudge thickens and starts to lose its glossy sheen. Add the chopped chocolate and nuts and stir until combined. Spoon the fudge into the prepared pan and spread level with a spatula.

Let cool completely then cut into squares and package into bags or boxes lined with waxed paper.

This will keep for 1 week if well wrapped and stored in an airtight container.

MAKES ABOUT 20 SQUARES

- sunflower oil, for greasing
- 2¼ cups superfine sugar
- scant ¾ cup evaporated milk
- ½ cup milk
- large pinch of salt
- ½ stick unsalted butter
- 2 teaspoons vanilla extract
- 3oz (75g) dark chocolate, chopped
- scant ½ cup chopped toasted almonds, hazelnuts, or pistachios

Ginger Snapdragon Cookies

Decorate the top of each of these extra gingery cookies with a small square of fine edible gold leaf which is available in small books from confectioners or baking suppliers.

Preheat the oven to 350°F (180°C) and line 2 baking sheets with nonstick parchment paper.

Cream together the softened butter and superfine sugar until light and fluffy. Add the corn syrup, molasses, and beaten egg and mix until smooth. Sift together the dry ingredients and stir into the mixture. Add the chopped stem ginger and mix again until thoroughly combined.

Using 2 spoons, place walnut-sized balls of the dough on the prepared baking sheets, spacing them well apart to allow enough space for them to spread during cooking. Bake in batches on the middle rack of the preheated oven for about 10–12 minutes, or until the cookies are golden brown—the edges should be crisp and the middle still slightly soft. Cool completely before packaging.

 Stored in an airtight box or cookie tin, these will keep for 4–5 days.

MAKES ABOUT 20 LARGE COOKIES

1 ¾ sticks unsalted butter, softened

generous ½ cup superfine sugar

½ cup corn syrup

scant ¼ cup molasses

1 large egg, beaten

scant 3½ cups self-rising flour

1 teaspoon baking soda

4–5 teaspoons ground ginger

large pinch of cayenne pepper

pinch of salt

2 nuggets of stem ginger, finely chopped

Slow-roasted Tomatoes

The long, slow cooking of these tomatoes capture the smell and taste of summer—then semi-preserves it in a jar. Using home-grown tomatoes would make this gift even more special. Try to use ripe, flavorful tomatoes, and nothing too large, as they will take much longer to cook. The cooking time will vary anyway, depending on the size of tomatoes used. Serve with bread and cheese, in a salad, or even in a pasta sauce.

Preheat the oven to 250°F (120°C).

Drizzle a large, shallow roasting pan with the olive oil. Cut the tomatoes into quarters and arrange in the pan, cut side uppermost. Sprinkle with the superfine sugar, oregano, and garlic. Scatter the thyme over the top, season with salt and pepper, and drizzle with more olive oil.

Cook the tomatoes on the middle rack of the preheated oven for around 3–5 hours, depending on the size of the tomatoes, until the skins have wrinkled and the tomato flesh has dried out. Turn the pan round a couple of times during the cooking so that the tomatoes cook evenly. You may need to start checking them after 4 hours, removing any smaller ones that are cooking quicker than the rest.

Pack the roasted tomatoes into a sterilized jar (see page 168) with some fresh basil leaves. Pour over extra virgin olive oil to cover and seal the jar.

 They will keep for up to 1 week in the refrigerator.

MAKES ABOUT 24
(2 X SMALL JARS)

2–3 tablespoons olive oil, plus extra for drizzling

10–12 smallish ripe tomatoes

1 teaspoon superfine sugar

1 teaspoon dried oregano

3 garlic cloves, peeled and sliced

2 sprigs of fresh thyme

1 teaspoon sea salt

sea salt and freshly ground black pepper

fresh basil leaves

2 cups extra virgin olive oil

Duck Confit

Duck confit will keep for weeks in a large glass jar so long as the meat is well covered in goose fat and the jar unopened, making it a perfect gift to include in a housewarming basket. The duck legs are first cured in salt, spices, and herbs and then cooked very slowly in goose fat until the meat is meltingly tender.

Arrange the duck legs in a single layer in a large ceramic or glass dish.

Put the garlic, salt, peppercorns, and juniper berries into a mortar and pound with a pestle until the peppercorns and juniper berries are very lightly crushed. Tear the bay leaves into small pieces and strip the leaves from the thyme sprig, then add to the mortar and stir well. Using your hands, rub the salt mixture all over the duck legs. Cover and chill for 24 hours, turning the legs over in the salt after 12 hours.

Preheat the oven to 300°F (150°C). Very quickly rinse the duck legs under cold water to remove the excess salt, then pat them dry on paper towels and lay them in a flameproof and ovenproof roasting pan or dish that will hold them snugly. Warm the goose fat over low heat and pour over the duck legs—they should be completely covered. Put the roasting pan on the stovetop, over low heat, until the fat reaches simmering point, then transfer to the middle rack of the preheated oven and cook for about 2 hours, until the meat is meltingly tender. You may need to turn the legs in the fat to ensure that they cook evenly.

Remove from the oven and let cool, then transfer the legs to a large sterilized jar (see page 168), pour over the goose fat so that they are completely covered, seal and store in the refrigerator until needed. Attach a label with the reheating instructions:

Preheat the oven to 425°F (220°C). Remove the duck legs from the container and scrape off almost all the goose fat. Roast skin side down on a solid baking sheet for 10 minutes, then drain off any excess fat. Turn the legs over and continue to cook for a further 10–15 minutes, until golden and crisp.

Make sure to attach a label with instructions for reheating and serving which should include a recipe for crispy sautéed potatoes, cooked in goose fat of course.

SERVES 6

6 duck legs

4 fat garlic cloves, peeled and sliced

6 rounded tablespoons coarse sea salt

1 teaspoon black peppercorns

2 juniper berries

2–3 bay leaves

1 large sprig of fresh thyme

3 x 12oz (340g) cans of goose fat

Tomato Chutney

No cheese sandwich is complete without a good dollop of chutney and this one packs a punch with a couple of red chili peppers and some generous spices. It would be a suitable rival to barbecue sauce for hamburgers or other grilled meats.

MAKES ABOUT 4 JARS

2¾lb (1.25kg) ripe tomatoes

2 onions

1 red bell pepper

1 apple (variety suitable for cooking)

2 large red chili peppers, seeded and finely chopped

2 fat garlic cloves, minced

1¼in. (3cm) piece of fresh ginger, grated

1 teaspoon black peppercorns

8 allspice berries

4 cardamom pods, bruised

2 cups white wine vinegar or cider vinegar

1 fresh bay leaf

1¾ cups soft light brown sugar

2 teaspoons black mustard seeds

salt and freshly ground black pepper

Using a small knife, make a cross on the bottom of each tomato. Place in a bowl, cover with boiling water, leave for 30 seconds to 1 minute to loosen the skins, then drain, and refresh under running cold water. Peel the tomatoes and roughly chop the flesh. Peel and finely chop the onions. Seed and dice the bell pepper. Peel, core, and dice the apple.

Put the chopped tomatoes, onions, and apples into a preserving saucepan or large saucepan. Add the chili peppers, garlic, and ginger. Wrap the peppercorns, allspice berries, and cardamom pods in a small square of cheesecloth, tie securely with kitchen string, and tie the end of the string to the saucepan handle so that the spices are submerged in the vegetables.

Pour over the vinegar, add the bay leaf, and bring to a boil, then reduce the heat and simmer gently for about 25–30 minutes, until the vegetables are tender. Add the sugar and stir to dissolve. Increase the heat slightly and simmer steadily until the chutney has reduced to a thick consistency. Add the mustard seeds and season with salt and freshly ground black pepper.

Remove the bay leaf and the cheesecloth spice bag, then spoon the chutney into warm sterilized jars (see page 168) and seal immediately. Let cool completely before labeling and storing.

Leave the chutney to mature for at least 4 weeks after bottling and before using. Once opened it should be stored in the refrigerator and used within 1 month.

Grissini really are easy to make and with a hint of fennel seed and chili pepper they are delicious to snack on or serve with dips.

Wrap a bundle of grissini sticks in a twist of waxed paper and give with a jar of Pesto (page 61) or Roasted Tomato Passata (page 90).

Fennel Seed, Chili Pepper, and Parmesan Grissini

MAKES ABOUT 25–30 GRISSINI

**2⅔ cups bread flour,
plus extra for dusting**

3 teaspoons active dry yeast

1 teaspoon sea salt

1 teaspoon fennel seeds, crushed

¼ teaspoon chili pepper flakes

generous ¾ cup–1 cup milk

3 tablespoons olive oil

**4 tablespoons finely grated
Parmesan cheese**

Place the flour, yeast, salt, fennel seeds, and chili pepper flakes into a large mixing bowl and make a well in the middle.

Warm the milk and pour it into the bowl along with the olive oil. Mix with a wooden spoon until the dough comes together. Add the Parmesan and mix until incorporated.

Lightly dust a work surface with a little flour, turn the dough out of the bowl and knead for about 5 minutes until smooth. Shape it into a ball and return the dough to the bowl. Cover with plastic wrap and leave in a warm, draft-free place for 1 hour until the dough has doubled in size.

Turn the dough out of the bowl and knead very lightly for 1 minute. Lightly dust the work surface again with flour and roll the dough out into a rectangle with a thickness of around ¼in. (5–7mm). Using a long sharp knife, cut the dough into strips just under ½in. (1cm) wide. Using your hands, quickly roll the strips one at a time to make them slightly more rounded and a little longer. Arrange on baking sheets, leaving space between the grissini.

Leave to rise again for another 15–20 minutes while you preheat the oven to 350°F (180°C). Cook the grissini sticks in batches on the middle rack of the preheated oven for 10–12 minutes, until crisp and golden brown. Leave until completely cold before packaging.

 Stored in an airtight container, these will keep for 4–5 days.

Tortellini with Roasted Butternut Squash, Spinach, and Ricotta

Preheat the oven to 350°F (180°C) and line a medium-size roasting pan with foil. Place the squash into the roasting pan and add the whole, unpeeled garlic. Drizzle with olive oil and season well with salt and freshly ground black pepper. Roast on the middle rack of the preheated oven for about 40–45 minutes, until the squash is tender.

Meanwhile cook the spinach. Place the leaves in a sauté pan with a splash of water and cook over medium heat for a couple of minutes, until wilted. Place in a strainer, and when cool enough to handle squeeze out any excess moisture with your hands. Finely chop the spinach and mix in a bowl with the ricotta, Pecorino Romano, and sage.

Remove the cooked squash from the oven and let cool slightly. Squeeze the garlic from its skins and blend in a food processor with the squash until smooth. Add to the spinach and cheese mixture, mix well, and season with salt and freshly ground black pepper. Set aside.

To make the pasta, place the flour in the bowl of a food processor, then add the beaten eggs and a pinch of salt. Pulse the mixture until it comes together into a ball—you may need to add a couple of teaspoons of cold water. Turn the dough out on to a lightly floured work surface and knead until smooth. Flatten into a disk, wrap in plastic wrap, and chill for at least 30 minutes.

Lightly dust the work surface with flour and roll out the pasta dough until it is about the thickness of a dime. Using a plain round cookie cutter with a diameter of about 3½in. (9cm), stamp out disks from the dough. Gather up the scraps, knead into a ball, re-roll, and stamp out more pasta disks. Arrange the disks on the work surface and spoon 1 rounded teaspoonful of filling into the top half of each. Lightly brush the edges with cold water, then fold over into a semi-circle, and press to seal. Bring the points of the semi-circle together and pinch.

Pack the fresh pasta in single layers into a box lined with waxed or parchment paper. Cover and label with the cooking instructions.

Cook in a large saucepan of boiling salted water for 2–3 minutes or until tender. Drain and toss with the very best extra virgin olive oil, homemade pesto, or passata and a good scattering of freshly grated Parmesan. These will keep for about 4 days if covered in the refrigerator.

Making these little tortellini is far easier than you'd imagine, so receiving a box of these little pasta parcels is a gift that most people would be impressed by. You don't need a pasta machine here but try to roll the pasta as thin as possible before stamping out the shapes.

Package into a shallow box lined with parchment paper and serve with a small jar of Pesto (page 61).

SERVES 4

1 medium-size butternut squash, peeled and cut into large chunks

4 garlic cloves

1–2 tablespoons olive oil

salt and freshly ground black pepper

3⅓ cups young leaf spinach

2 tablespoons ricotta cheese

2 tablespoons grated Pecorino Romano cheese

2 teaspoons chopped fresh sage

2⅔ cups pizza flour or '00' flour, plus extra for dusting

3 large eggs, lightly beaten

Passata

Passata is made from ripe tomatoes that have been puréed and strained to remove the skin and seeds. If you grow your own tomatoes then making homemade passata is the perfect way to use up an abundance of your crop. It's almost like bottling a little bit of summer that you can use throughout the year. Why not package a bottle of passata with a box of homemade tortellini (see page 88) and a bundle of grissini (see page 87) to give as a housewarming gift or to the lover of all things Italian?

Preheat the oven to 350°F (180°C).

Halve the tomatoes and put into a large roasting pan. Peel the onions and cut into wedges. Trim and slice the celery, and peel and roughly chop the carrot. Add everything to the pan along with the unpeeled garlic cloves. Quarter and seed the red bell peppers and add to the pan.

Drizzle with the oil and vinegar and add the oregano sprig. Sprinkle over the sugar and chili pepper and season well with salt and freshly ground black pepper. Cover loosely with foil and roast on the middle rack of the oven for about 45 minutes, or until the vegetables are tender.

Remove the pan from the oven and pop the garlic cloves from their skins. Peel the skin from the red bell peppers and discard the oregano. Place the roasted vegetables in a food processor and blend until smooth. Taste and check the seasoning, adding more salt and pepper or a pinch of sugar if needed. Add the chopped fresh basil and pour the hot passata into clean, sterilized jars (see page 168). Let cool before labeling.

Passata will keep for 2–3 months if unopened. Once opened, store in the refrigerator and use within 3–4 days.

MAKES 2–3 LARGE JARS

3lb 5oz (1.5kg) ripe tomatoes

2 small onions

1 stick of celery

1 medium carrot

1 whole head of garlic

2 red bell peppers

6 tablespoons extra virgin olive oil

splash of balsamic vinegar

1 bushy sprig of fresh oregano

3 teaspoons superfine sugar

pinch of chili pepper flakes

salt and freshly ground black pepper

2 tablespoons chopped fresh basil

Pickled Shallots

You will need to prepare these pickled shallots at least a month before you plan on giving them away, to allow the delicious spiced vinegar to work its magic.

MAKES 2 LARGE JAM JARS

18oz (500g) small shallots

2oz (50g) sea salt

2 cups white wine vinegar

1 rounded tablespoon light muscovado sugar

1 bay leaf

4 allspice berries

pinch of chili pepper flakes

½ teaspoon coriander seeds

½ teaspoon mustard seeds

4 black peppercorns

Peel the shallots, leaving them whole and the root end attached. The easiest way to do this is to place the shallots in a bowl, cover with boiling water and leave them for 2–3 minutes to soften the skins. Then drain and peel them, using a small sharp knife. Dissolve the sea salt in 2 cups water in a ceramic bowl, add the peeled shallots, cover, and let soak for 24 hours.

While the shallots are soaking, prepare the spiced vinegar. Pour the vinegar into a stainless steel saucepan, add the sugar and spices, and place the saucepan over medium heat, stirring occasionally until the sugar has dissolved. Slowly bring to a boil, then reduce the heat and simmer very gently for 10 minutes. Remove from the heat and let the vinegar cool.

Drain the shallots, rinse well in cold water, and pat dry on paper towels.

Pack the shallots into sterilized jars (see page 168) and pour over the spiced vinegar, making sure that the shallots are completely covered. Seal the jars and label.

This is definitely one for the boys! Serve as part of a tasty lunch with man-sized hunks of crusty bread and a wedge of tangy hard cheese. Store in a cool, dark place for at least 1 month before opening. Once opened, use within 1 month.

Pickled Beets

Banish all thoughts of over-vinegary pickled beets here. These beet wedges are packed into a slightly sweet and spiced vinegar. Squirrel the jars away in a cool cupboard until Christmas when they'd be perfect to take to any holiday lunch to eat with cold cuts of meat.

This is another great recipe that's ideal for gardeners when faced with an unexpectedly large crop of beets.

Wash the beets and put them into a saucepan. Cover with cold water and add the salt. Bring to a boil, then reduce the heat, and cook at a gentle simmer until the beets are tender when tested with the point of a small sharp knife.

While the beets are cooking, prepare the spiced vinegar. Put both vinegars into a saucepan with the sugar, cinnamon, star anise, coriander, mustard seeds, and peppercorns. Set over low to medium heat until the sugar has dissolved, then bring slowly to a boil. Simmer for 2–3 minutes and remove from the heat.

When the beets are cooked, drain them and set aside until cool enough to handle. Peel off the skins and cut each beets into 6 or 8 wedges through the root. Reheat the spiced vinegar until just boiling. Add the beets, shallots, and garlic, simmer for 1 minute, then remove from the heat.

Using a slotted spoon, remove the beet wedges from the liquid and pack into the sterilized jars (see page 168). Pour over the spiced vinegar to cover the beets and immediately seal. Let cool before labeling.

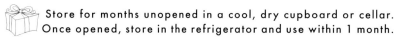 Store for months unopened in a cool, dry cupboard or cellar. Once opened, store in the refrigerator and use within 1 month.

MAKES 2 LARGE JAM JARS

18oz (500g) whole beets (approx. 4 medium beets)

1 teaspoon sea salt

1¼ cups malt vinegar

⅓ cup balsamic vinegar

⅓ cup light muscovado or soft light brown sugar

1 cinnamon stick

2 star anise

1 teaspoon coriander seeds

1 teaspoon mustard seeds

4–5 black peppercorns

2 small shallots or 1 large, peeled and sliced

2 garlic cloves, peeled and sliced

Damson or Plum Cheese

"Cheese" is a bit of a misnomer here. This is really a damson paste that is quite delicious when served with cheese in much the same way as Membrillo (or quince paste) is traditionally eaten with Manchego cheese.

MAKES ABOUT 4 SMALL JARS

2¼lb (1kg) damsons
approx. 3⅓ cups superfine sugar
juice of ¼–½ a lemon

Rinse the damsons under cold running water and place in a large saucepan with ⅔ cup of water. Cover and cook over low heat until the fruit is very tender, and the flesh has come away from the stones and cooked down to a thick pulp. Remove the saucepan from the heat and push the damsons through a nylon sieve into a clean bowl.

Scoop the purée into a measuring cup and make a note of the amount. For every 2½ cups of damson purée you will need 2 cups of superfine sugar and a small squeeze of lemon juice.

Put the damson purée, the correct weight of sugar, and the lemon juice into a solid-bottomed sauté saucepan or saucepan and set over low to medium heat. Cook the mixture very gently at first to dissolve the sugar, then continue to cook, stirring regularly, until it becomes a thick paste—it should have the consistency of lightly whipped cream.

Pour the damson cheese into small, straight-sided sterilized jars (see page 168) and seal immediately. Label the jars once completely cold.

Store for months unopened in a cool, dark cupboard or cellar. Once opened, store in the refrigerator well wrapped in plastic wrap and use within 1 month.

Damson or Plum Vodka

After you have strained off the damsons from the vodka the resulting fruit could be added to a boozy crumble if you're feeling brave!

Rinse the damsons under cold running water. Prick each damson 4 or 5 times with a fork and place them in a sterilized (see page 168), wide-necked preserving jar with a capacity of 8 cups.

Add the superfine sugar, cinnamon stick, and lemon zest and pour over the vodka. Secure the lid and give the jar a good shake to dissolve the sugar. Leave in a cool, dry, dark place for at least 3 months, shaking the jar at least once a week or every time you walk past.

After 3 months the vodka will be a deep plum color and deeply flavored by the damsons. Taste and add more sugar if desired. Strain the vodka through a colander into a large bowl. Strain again, either through cheesecloth or paper coffee filters, into sterilized bottles (see page 168). Seal the bottles with sterilized stoppers and attach labels.

 This never lasts for long in my house, but will keep forever in reality.

MAKES 1 LARGE BOTTLE

18oz (500g) damsons
generous ½ cup superfine sugar
1 cinnamon stick
pared zest of 1 organic lemon
1 x 25fl oz (750ml) bottle of good-quality vodka

WINTER

CHAPTER 4

Cheese Sablés

Buttery, crumbly, cheesey, just a little spicy and absolutely perfect with a glass of chilled white wine. Coat the outside of these cookies with a mixture of sesame and kalonji seeds to make them a more sophisticated cocktail nibble.

Combine the flour, salt, cayenne, mustard powder, cumin or caraway seeds, and some black pepper into the bowl of a food processor. Add the diced butter and use the pulse button to rub it into the dry ingredients. Add the grated cheeses and pulse again until the dough just comes together—you may need to add a drop of cold water.

Turn the dough out onto a lightly floured work surface and roll into a log roughly 2in. (5cm) in diameter, wrap in plastic wrap and chill in the fridge for a few hours, or until firm.

Preheat the oven to 350°F (180°C) and line a baking sheet with nonstick parchment paper. Take the log out of the fridge, remove the plastic wrap and brush with milk before coating in the sesame and kalonji seeds (if using). Slice the log into disks, roughly ¼in. (5mm) thick, and arrange on the baking sheets, spacing the cookies well apart.

Bake on the middle rack of the preheated oven for 12–15 minutes, or until crisp and golden. Once completely cold, the sablés can be packaged.

 Stored in an airtight container, they will keep for 4–5 days.

MAKES ABOUT 24

1⅓ cups all-purpose flour, plus extra for dusting

1 teaspoon sea salt

½ teaspoon cayenne pepper

½ teaspoon dry mustard powder

1 teaspoon cumin or caraway seeds, lightly crushed

1⅓ sticks unsalted butter, chilled and diced

⅔ cup finely grated sharp Cheddar cheese

¾ cup finely grated Parmesan cheese

1 tablespoon milk

sesame seeds (optional)

kalonji (black onion) seeds (optional)

freshly ground black pepper

Wholegrain Honey Mustard

This recipe is incredibly easy to make, but will, of course, be influenced by the quality of the ingredients you use. I have suggested using white wine vinegar, but you could look for specialty vinegars that use specific grape varieties.

Mix the mustard seeds, chili pepper flakes, vinegar, and cinnamon together in a bowl. Cover and set aside for at least 12 hours and up to 24.

Remove and discard the cinnamon stick from the mustard seeds, add the honey, and mix well. Transfer three-quarters of the mixture to either a food processor and blend until lightly crushed or pound the mustard using a mortar and pestle.

Combine with the remaining soaked mustard seeds and season with salt. Spoon into sterilized jars (see page 168), cover, and seal before labelling.

 Store for months unopened in a cool, dry cupboard or pantry. Once opened, it will keep for 2–3 months in the fridge.

MAKES 3 JARS

2 cups mixed yellow and brown mustard seeds

1 teaspoon chili pepper flakes

1¼ cups white wine vinegar or cider vinegar

1 cinnamon stick

¼ cup honey

1 teaspoon sea salt

This mustard is perfect when served with with a variety of cold meats, in sandwiches, or, quite simply, with homemade oatmeal biscuits (see page 120) and marinated goat cheese (see page 58).

Limoncello

This after-dinner drink is like a little ray of boozy citrus sunshine at the end of a heavy meal and should be served very cold, in little shot glasses. If you're lucky enough to find some lemons with stems and leaves attached, these would make a very beautiful label or gift tag.

Wash and dry the lemons and remove the zest in fine strips, using a vegetable peeler. Squeeze the juice from the lemons and set aside. Pour ⅓ cup of water into a small pan, add the zest and sugar, and slowly bring to a boil, stirring occasionally until the sugar has dissolved. Reduce the heat and simmer very gently for 15 minutes. Add the lemon juice and simmer for another 5 minutes. Remove from the heat and set aside to cool.

Pour the vodka into a large sterilized preserving jar (see page 168) and add the lemony syrup. Secure the lid and shake well. Set aside in a cool, dry, dark place for a week, shaking the jar every day. Strain off the lemon zest and decant the limoncello into a pretty bottle.

 This will keep for months.

MAKES 1 X 25fl oz (750ml) BOTTLE

6 organic lemons
1¼ cups superfine sugar
1 x 25fl oz (750ml) bottle of good-quality vodka

Chocolate Truffles

You may need to make up two batches of these truffles—one to give away and one to keep for yourself. I have given a number of flavor options that can be added to the basic recipe, but if you prefer, you can simply add a couple of tablespoons of your favorite liqueur. The rolled truffles are coated in crisp dark chocolate but are just as delicious when simply dusted with cocoa.

Line a baking sheet with nonstick parchment paper.

Put the cream, sugar, and salt into a pan over medium heat. Bring to a boil, stirring to dissolve the sugar, then reduce the heat and simmer very gently for 1 minute. Put the chopped chocolate in a bowl. Remove the pan from the heat and pour the mixture over the chocolate. Stir until the chocolate has melted and the mixture is smooth.

Divide the mixture evenly between 2 bowls and add whichever flavor you have chosen (see below). Mix thoroughly, then leave to cool and set in the fridge for about 2 hours.

Scoop 1 teaspoonful of set truffle mixture into the palm of your hand. Roll it quickly into a ball and place on the lined baking sheet. Repeat with the remaining mixture. Chill the truffles until firm.

To temper the chocolate for coating the truffles, place 4oz (100g) of the finely chopped chocolate in a small bowl set over a pan of barely simmering water. The bottom of the bowl should not come into contact with the water or the chocolate will scorch. Stir the chocolate until melted and smooth. Remove the bowl from the pan and add the remaining 2oz (50g) of chopped chocolate. Stir until melted and thoroughly combined and the chocolate has cooled and thickened slightly. Return the bowl to the pan and warm the tempered chocolate over the water once more. It is now ready to use.

First, lay out a clean sheet of parchment paper. Taking 1 truffle at a time, drop it into the tempered chocolate. Using a fork and working quickly, roll the truffle to coat it in the chocolate, then lift it and allow the excess to drip back into the bowl, tapping the tines of the fork on the edge. Carefully slide the truffle off the fork on to the clean parchment paper. Repeat with the remaining truffles and leave to harden before packaging into pretty boxes.

 Stored in a cool place, truffles will keep for up to one week. If kept in the fridge, bring them out 30 minutes before serving.

MAKES ABOUT 35 TRUFFLES

TRUFFLES:

¾ cup heavy cream

½ cup light muscovado sugar

pinch of sea salt

9oz (250g) best-quality dark chocolate, finely chopped

TO COAT:

6oz (150g) best-quality dark chocolate, finely chopped

FLAVOR VARIATIONS

CANDIED ORANGE

1oz (25g) candied orange peel, finely chopped

STEM GINGER

1oz (25g) stem ginger in syrup, drained and finely chopped

CHERRY AND COCONUT

⅓ cup shredded coconut, lightly toasted

2oz (50g) dried morello cherries, chopped

Mango Chutney with Chili Pepper and Ginger

A perfect accompaniment for any Indian meal, served with a stack of freshly cooked poppadums and warm naan bread. Or equally good on a picnic, spooned onto crusty bread and eaten with some tangy cheese.

Place the onions, garlic, chili pepper, and ginger in a preserving pan. Cut the apple and mangoes into ½in. (1cm) chunks and add to the pan.

Crack the cardamom pods using a mortar and pestle, extract the seeds, and discard the green husks. Toast the cardamom, fenugreek, cumin, and coriander seeds in a dry frying pan until toasted and fragrant and lightly grind in the mortar and pestle. Toast the mustard seeds in the same frying pan and add to the preserving pan, along with the lightly ground spices, cinnamon stick, and ground turmeric.

Add the vinegar, black onion seeds, and salt and bring slowly to a boil. Continue to cook over medium heat until the apple and mango is pulpy, stirring from time to time. Add both sugars and continue to cook for about 30 minutes, until the mixture has thickened, reduced, and the fruit is very soft but still chunky.

Add the lime juice to give the chutney a little extra pep, stir to combine, and remove the pan from the heat. Remove the cinnamon stick, spoon into sterilized jars (see page 168), and seal immediately.

Once the chutney is completely cold, label the jars, and store in a cool, dark place for 4 weeks before serving.

 Store for months, unopened, in a cool, dark cupboard or pantry. Once opened, store in the fridge and use within 1 month.

MAKES 4 X 1lb (450g) JARS

2 onions, peeled and finely chopped

3 fat garlic cloves, peeled and finely chopped

1 red chili pepper, seeded and finely chopped

1½in. (4cm) piece of fresh ginger, peeled and finely grated

1 Macintosh apple, peeled, cored and quartered

juice of 1 lime

4 large ripe mangoes, peeled and pitted

4 cardamom pods

1 teaspoon fenugreek seeds

1 teaspoon cumin seeds

½ teaspoon coriander seeds

2 teaspoons black mustard seeds

1 cinnamon stick

½ teaspoon ground turmeric

1½ cups white wine vinegar

1⅓ cups light brown sugar

1 cup golden granulated sugar

1 teaspoon kalonji (black onion) seeds

1 teaspoon salt

Spiced Cranberry Jelly

This jelly makes a delicious alternative to cranberry sauce and would be a welcome addition to any Christmas or Thanksgiving dinner.

MAKES 3–4 SMALL
JAM JARS

1¼lb (1kg) fresh cranberries
2 oranges
1 cinnamon stick
5 whole cloves
2 star anise
approx. 2½ cups granulated sugar

Place the cranberries in a preserving pan or large saucepan. Remove the zest from the oranges using a vegetable peeler and add to the pan with the squeezed orange juice, the cinnamon stick, cloves, and star anise. Add 1⅓ cups water, cover the pan, and set over medium heat to simmer gently for 20–30 minutes, until the cranberries are very tender and have burst.

Remove from the heat and pour the contents of the pan through a jelly bag suspended over a large bowl or pan. Let the cranberries drip through the bag for at least 4 hours, or overnight, but do not be tempted to stir or push them through or the resulting jelly will be cloudy.

The next day, pour the strained cranberry juice into a measuring cup and make a note of the quantity. For every 2 cups of juice you will need 2¼ cups of granulated sugar. Return the juice to a clean pan, then add the sugar, and stir over low heat, until it has dissolved. Increase the heat and boil steadily until setting point is reached (see page 168).

Pour the jelly into sterilized jars (see page 168) and seal immediately. Label the jars once the jelly is completely cold.

 Store for months, unopened, in a cool, dark cupboard or pantry. Once opened, store in the fridge and use within 1 month.

Piccalilli

Piccalilli is one of those old-fashioned types of pickle that I think no picnic or camping trip should be without. It's packed full of crisp vegetables that are all bound together in a bright, turmeric mustard yellow sauce and is the perfect partner to pot pies, cold cuts, and hearty cheese sarnies.

Prepare the vegetables, and try to cut them into similar-sized pieces. Cut the cauliflower into small florets. Peel the carrots and cut into thick batons or chunks. Trim the French and runner beans and cut into 1in. (2cm) lengths. Cut the cucumber in half lengthwise and scoop out the seeds. Cut the cucumber and zucchini into chunks. Peel the onions.

Put all the vegetables into a large ceramic or plastic bowl. Dissolve the salt in 5 cups of cold water and pour over the prepared vegetables. Cover and leave overnight in a cool place.

Put the vinegar, bay leaf, mustard seeds, peppercorns, coriander seeds, allspice berries, and whole garlic cloves into a large nonreactive pan. Bring to a boil, then reduce the heat, and simmer very gently for 5–10 minutes. Remove from the heat and leave to cool—this will allow the seasonings to infuse into the vinegar.

In a bowl, mix together the flour, mustard powder, turmeric, and ginger. Add 2–3 tablespoons of the spiced vinegar and mix to a paste. Strain in the remaining vinegar and pour back into the pan. Add the sugar and bring to a boil, stirring constantly, until slightly thickened. The sauce should be glossy and thick enough to coat the back of a spoon.

Drain the vegetables, rinse briefly under cold water, and pat dry on paper towels. Add to the hot vinegar mixture and cook over low heat for 4–5 minutes, until just tender. Spoon into hot sterilized jars (see page 168) and cover immediately. Once cold, label and store in a cool dark cupboard for about 3 weeks before using.

 Store for months, unopened, in a cool, dark cupboard or pantry. Once opened, store in the fridge and use within 1 month.

MAKES 3 X 1lb JARS

- 1 small cauliflower
- 2 medium carrots
- ¼lb (125g) French beans
- ¼lb (125g) runner beans
- ½ cucumber
- 1 zucchini
- 10 silverskin onions
- 1 cup sea salt
- 2½ cups white malt vinegar
- 1 bay leaf
- 2 teaspoons yellow mustard seeds
- 8 black peppercorns
- ½ teaspoon coriander seeds
- 3 allspice berries
- 2 garlic cloves, peeled
- ⅔ cup all-purpose flour
- 1 tablespoon English mustard powder
- 2 teaspoons ground turmeric
- 1 teaspoon ground ginger
- ⅓ cup superfine sugar

Chocolate-coated Candied Almonds

One batch of these almonds will make enough to package into more than one gift. Although they are delicious when simply candied with their coating of sugar and cinnamon, once they are dipped in dark chocolate and given a light dusting of cocoa they become something else altogether. Package the almonds into screw-top jars tied with ribbons.

Preheat the oven to 300°F (150°C) and line a medium-sized baking sheet with nonstick parchment paper.

Combine the sugar, cinnamon, salt, and almonds in a bowl. In a second bowl, whisk the egg white until foamy. Add the vanilla extract, then the almond and sugar mixture, and stir to coat the nuts evenly.

Turn out onto the baking sheet and spread in an even layer. Bake on the middle rack of the oven for about 30 minutes, until crisp, turning the nuts a couple of times. Remove from the oven and leave to cool on the baking sheet.

Once they are completely cold, coat the nuts in chocolate and cocoa. Break the chocolate into pieces and melt it in a heatproof bowl set over a pan of barely simmering water or in the microwave on a low setting. Stir until smooth and leave to cool slightly. Taking a few almonds at a time, dip them into the chocolate, allowing any excess to drip back into the bowl.

Leave the chocolate-coated almonds to set on the parchment paper, then dust them with cocoa and package them into boxes or bags.

These will keep for about 2 weeks in a jar or airtight container.

MAKES 2 JAM JARS

½ cup golden superfine sugar
2 teaspoons ground cinnamon
pinch of salt
1⅓ cups whole almonds
1 medium egg white
1 teaspoon vanilla extract
7oz (200g) dark chocolate
1–2 tablespoons cocoa, for dusting

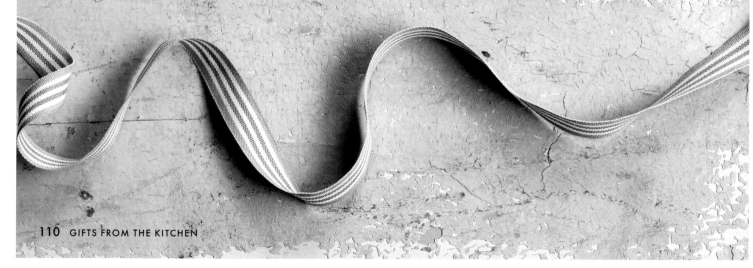

Florentines

A box of delicate jeweled Florentine cookies dipped in white and dark chocolate would be a sophisticated and irresistable box of goodies to give to any hostess.

Preheat the oven to 350°F (180°C) and line 2 solid baking sheets with nonstick parchment paper.

Finely chop the candied peel and quarter the candied cherries. Chop the blanched almonds or pistachios. Mix the fruit and nuts together in a medium-sized bowl and set aside.

Melt the butter, superfine sugar, and honey in a small pan over low heat, stirring constantly to prevent the sugar from sticking on the bottom of the pan. Remove from the heat and add the flour, ground ginger, and salt. Stir until smooth, then add the cream and stir again. Pour on to the fruit and nuts and stir well to combine.

Spoon rounded teaspoons of the mixture on to the prepared baking sheets, leaving plenty of space between the mounds. Bake on the middle rack of the preheated oven for about 10 minutes, or until the edges of the Florentines are golden brown. Remove from the oven and leave to cool on the baking sheets until crisp.

Melt the chocolates separately in heatproof bowls over pans of barely simmering water. Spread the underside of each Florentine with either dark or white chocolate and leave until the chocolate has hardened before packaging in single layers between sheets of waxed or nonstick paper.

 Florentines will keep for 4–5 days in an airtight container.

MAKES 24 FLORENTINES

2½oz (75g) mixed candied peel
2½oz (75g) candied cherries
½ cup blanched almonds
¼ cup unsalted pistachios or slivered almonds
¼ stick unsalted butter
¼ cup superfine sugar
1 tablespoon honey
3 tablespoons all-purpose flour
pinch of ground ginger
pinch of salt
2 tablespoons heavy cream
3½oz (100g) dark chocolate
3½oz (100g) white chocolate

Biscotti with Almonds and Figs

Biscotti are so easy to make and take no time at all to prepare. Tie up bundles of biscotti with beautiful ribbons and package with a set of vintage espresso cups or perhaps a bottle of Vin Santo.

Preheat the oven to 350°F (180°C). Melt the butter in the microwave or in a small pan and cool slightly.

Sift the flour, sugar, salt, and baking powder into a large mixing bowl. Add the chopped almonds, figs, and lemon zest and mix well with a wooden spoon.

In a small bowl, whisk together the whole egg, egg yolk, vanilla extract, and cooled melted butter. Make a well in the middle of the dry ingredients and pour the egg and butter mixture into it. Stir until the ingredients are thoroughly combined and come together into a ball.

Divide the biscotti dough into two equal pieces. Very lightly dust a work surface with a little all-purpose flour and roll the dough into 2 logs, each about 8in. (20cm) long. Cover a baking sheet with parchment paper and place the logs on the paper, leaving plenty of space between them.

Bake on the middle rack of the preheated oven for about 35–40 minutes, until golden brown and firm to the touch. Remove from the oven and leave to cool on the baking tray. Turn off the oven.

When the logs are completely cold, preheat the oven to 325°F (170°C) and cover 2 baking sheets with nonstick parchment paper. Using a long, sharp knife, slice the biscotti logs on the diagonal into slices no thicker than ½in. (1cm) thick, and arrange in a single layer on the baking sheets.

Bake on the middle rack of the oven for about 20 minutes, until crisp. You may need to swap the sheets around and turn the biscotti over halfway through baking. Cool and package into cellophane bags or pretty boxes.

 Stored in an airtight container, these will keep for about a week.

MAKES ABOUT 24

½ **stick unsalted butter**

2 **cups all-purpose flour, plus a little extra for rolling**

¾ **cup superfine sugar**

pinch of salt

½ **teaspoon baking powder**

⅔ **cup whole almonds, roughly chopped**

3½oz (100g) **dried figs (or dried morello cherries), roughly chopped**

finely grated zest of ½ **an organic lemon**

1 **large egg**

1 **large egg yolk**

1 **teaspoon vanilla extract**

Chocolate and Ginger Loaf Cake

I always think that if you're going to make the effort to bake a cake you might as well make two while you have the oven on. That way you can spread the love and give a chocolate cake to two lucky friends. If you prefer, you can swap the stem ginger for candied peel or chocolate chips.

MAKES 2 X 1lb (500g) CAKES

3½oz (100g) dark chocolate, chopped

2 nuggets of stem ginger, in syrup

¾ cup all-purpose flour

½ cup cocoa

½ teaspoon baking powder

1 teaspoon baking soda

¼ cup ground almonds

pinch of salt

½ cup sour cream

⅓ cup sunflower oil

2 large eggs

1 cup light brown sugar

¼ cup boiling water

CHOCOLATE GANACHE:

7oz (200g) dark chocolate (72% cacoa solids)

⅔ stick unsalted butter

2 tablespoons heavy cream

Preheat the oven to 350°F (180°C). Butter and line the bottoms and sides of 2 x 1lb (500g) loaf pans with a strip of buttered parchment paper.

Melt the chocolate either in a heatproof bowl set over a pan of barely simmering water or in the microwave on a low setting. Stir until smooth and set aside. Finely chop the stem ginger.

Sift together the flour, cocoa, baking powder, baking soda, ground almonds, and salt. Mix together the sour cream and sunflower oil.

In the bowl of an electric mixer and using the whisk attachment, beat the eggs and sugar until they are pale and thick and the mixture leaves a ribbon trail when the beater is lifted from the mixture. Stir in the melted chocolate and chopped ginger.

Add the sifted dry ingredients, then the oil and sour cream, and fold into the cake mixture until smooth. Whisk in the boiling water, stir until smooth, and divide the mixture between the prepared cake pans. Bake on the middle rack of the preheated oven for 35 minutes, or until a wooden skewer inserted into the middle of the cakes comes out clean.

Cool the cakes in the pans for 10 minutes, then transfer to a wire rack until completely cold.

To make the ganache, melt together the chocolate, butter, and heavy cream either in a heatproof bowl set over a pan of barely simmering water or in a microwave on a low setting. Stir until smooth and combined. Set aside to cool and thicken slightly.

Using an offset spatula, spread the ganache over the top of each cake and allow to set before decorating with chopped nuts and stem ginger.

 Stored in an airtight container, this will keep for 4–5 days.

Spiced Nuts

Fill homemade paper cones with spoonfuls of these mixed spiced nuts. They're the perfect little package to give to the cocktail enthusiast in your life, along with a bottle of the Chili Pepper Vodka (page 167).

Preheat the oven to 350°F (180°C).

Place all the nuts and seeds into a large bowl and drizzle the olive oil and honey over the top. Add the salt and spices and a generous grinding of black pepper. Mix well to coat the nuts evenly in the spices. Turn the mixture out onto a large baking sheet and spread evenly.

Roast on the middle rack of the preheated oven for about 10 minutes, stirring the mixture regularly so that it browns evenly. When the nuts are golden, remove from the oven and allow to cool before packaging into paper cones to serve.

 These nuts will keep for 3 days in an airtight container.

MAKES 8 PAPER CONES

5¼ cups mixed nuts (Brazils, walnuts, pecans, almonds, cashews, peanuts, and macadamias)

¼ cup pumpkin seeds

⅓ cup sunflower seeds

2 tablespoons olive oil

2 tablespoons honey

2 teaspoons sea salt flakes

2 teaspoons cumin seeds, coarsely ground

1½ teaspoons paprika

1 rounded teaspoon celery salt

freshly ground black pepper

Pecan Snowball Cookies

Dusted with a generous scattering of confectioners' (icing) sugar, these crumbly, buttery Snowball Cookies are scrumptious with a cup of tea for a mid-morning snack.

Preheat the oven to 325°F (150°C) and line 2 baking sheets with nonstick parchment paper.

Toast the pecans in the preheated oven for 5–7 minutes. Leave to cool, then chop in a food processor until finely ground.

Cream the softened butter and confectioners' (icing) sugar until pale, light, and fluffy. Add the vanilla extract and mix again. Sift the flour, baking powder, and salt into the bowl, add the ground pecans and mix until smooth and thoroughly combined. Cover the cookie dough and chill for 30 minutes to allow it to firm up.

Roll teaspoons of the cookie dough into balls and arrange on the baking sheets, spacing them well apart. Bake in batches on the middle rack of the preheated oven for about 15 minutes, until pale golden. Remove the cookies from the oven and cool slightly.

Dust the cookies liberally with confectioners' (icing) sugar and package into pretty bags or boxes once completely cold.

 Stored in an airtight container, cookies will keep for 5 days.

MAKES 24 COOKIES

1⅓ cups pecans

1⅓ sticks unsalted butter, softened

1 cup confectioners' (icing) sugar

1 teaspoon vanilla extract

2 cups all-purpose flour

½ teaspoon baking powder

large pinch of salt

confectioners' (icing) sugar, for dusting

Herbal Teas

MAKES 20 TEA BAGS

SLEEPY TEA:

dried camomile
dried lemon balm
dried passiflora
dried rose buds or petals

DE-STRESS TEA:

dried camomile
dried lemon balm
dried lime blossoms
dried passiflora
dried skullcap

Give a box of these herbal tea bags with a beautiful vintage teapot. Ready-to-fill tea bags are available from health food stores or online—fill them with your selected blend and attach a handmade label to each bag. Alternatively, present the loose tea in glass jars or tea caddies, and include instructions for making a brew using a mesh strainer.

Combine equal quantities (2oz/50g) of each of the dried herbs in a bowl and mix well. Scoop 1 heaping teaspoon of the blend into each tea bag, tie with fine string or thread, and attach a pretty label to each bag.

 Stored in an airtight container, these will keep for at least 3 months.

Oatmeal Crackers for Cheese

These crackers are perfect to serve with all types of cheese, but are particularly delicious when served with some homemade chutney or relish, too. There are many different whole-wheat flours now available, so play around with different types to see which you prefer. I particularly like using a flour with wheat and barley flakes, kibbled rye, and assorted seeds already added.

Sift the oat bran, flour, baking powder, mustard powder, pepper, and salt into a large bowl and add any bran left in the sifter. Pour into the bowl of a food processor and add the diced butter and superfine sugar.

Using the pulse button, process the mixture until the butter has been rubbed into the flour. Add the milk and pulse again until the mixture comes together to form a dough. Put it on to a flour-dusted work surface and knead very lightly and just enough to bring it together. Cover with a clean cloth and set aside for 15 minutes.

Meanwhile, preheat the oven to 350°F (180°C) and line 2 baking sheets with nonstick parchment paper.

Lightly flour the work surface again, then roll the dough to about ¼in (5mm) thickness and cut out shapes, using a cookie cutter. Reroll any trimmings. Prick the biscuits with a fork, arrange on the prepared baking sheets and bake on the middle rack of the preheated oven for about 12 minutes, or until starting to turn golden at the edges. You may need to swap the baking sheets around halfway through cooking.

Cool the crackers on the baking sheets for 2 minutes, then transfer them to a wire cooling rack.

 Stored in an airtight tin, these crackers will keep for a couple of weeks.

MAKES 25–30 CRACKERS

⅔ cup oat bran or oatmeal

1⅓ cups whole-wheat flour

2 level teaspoons baking powder

1 teaspoon dried mustard powder

½ teaspoon freshly ground black pepper

1 teaspoon sea salt

1 stick unsalted butter, diced and chilled

2 level tablespoons golden superfine sugar

3 tablespoons milk

all-purpose flour, for rolling

Shortbreads

Here is one basic recipe that can be adapted to make a myriad of shortbread flavors. Shortbread always reminds me of my childhood, since we always had a box of assorted flavors on hand for the holidays.

To make the shortbread dough, cream the softened butter and confectioners' (icing) sugar until pale and light. Add the vanilla extract and mix again. Sift the flour (cocoa, if using for the chocolate shortbread) and salt, add to the mixture, and beat until smooth. Flatten the dough into a disk, wrap in plastic wrap, and chill until firm.

Preheat the oven to 350°F (180°C) and line a baking sheet with nonstick parchment paper. Lightly dust the work surface with all-purpose flour and roll the dough out to a thickness of about a quarter. Using cookie cutters, stamp out shapes and arrange on the baking sheet.

Bake on the middle rack of the preheated oven for around 12–15 minutes, until crisp and pale golden. Cool on the baking sheets, then package into pretty boxes or bags.

MAKES ABOUT 24 IN TOTAL

VANILLA SHORTBREAD:

2 sticks unsalted butter, softened

¾ cup confectioners' (icing) sugar, sifted

1 teaspoon vanilla extract

2 cups all-purpose flour, plus extra for rolling

pinch of salt

CHOCOLATE SHORTBREAD:

2 sticks unsalted butter, softened

¾ cup confectioners' (icing) sugar, sifted

1 teaspoon vanilla extract

2 cups all-purpose flour, plus extra for rolling

⅔ cup cocoa

pinch of salt

VARIATIONS

Pistachio Chocolate-dipped Shortbread
Add 1 cup of finely chopped unsalted, shelled pistachios to the shortbread mixture (chocolate or vanilla). Stamp out disks of shortbread and bake. Spread the baked and cooled shortbread discs with melted dark chocolate and scatter with chopped pistachios.

Stem Ginger Shortbread
Add 1 teaspoon of ground ginger and 1 finely chopped nugget of stem ginger to the basic vanilla mixture.

Lemon Shortbread
Add the finely grated zest of 1 organic lemon, 1 teaspoon of lemon extract, and 1 tablespoon of finely chopped candied lemon peel to the vanilla shortbread mixture in place of the vanilla extract.

Almond Shortbread
Add 1 cup finely chopped or ground almonds to the chocolate or vanilla mixture.

Hazelnut Shortbread
Add 1 cup finely chopped or ground hazelnuts to the chocolate or vanilla mixture.

Morello Cherry Shortbread
Add 1 cup chopped dried morello cherries to the vanilla or chocolate mixture.

CELEBRATIONS

CHAPTER 5

Fortune Cookies

Fill each of these cookies with a personalized message of goodwill and give them to your family and friends for the New Year or any other significant event. Bake the cookies in small quantities, since you have to work very quickly to fill and shape them once they come out of the oven before the delicate mixture becomes dry, brittle, and impossible to fold.

Preheat the oven to 300°F (150°C) and line 2 baking sheets with nonstick parchment paper.

Sift together the flour, ground ginger, and salt. In a medium-sized bowl, whisk the egg whites until foamy. Add the confectioners' (icing) sugar and vanilla extract and whisk until combined. Stir in the sifted dry ingredients, then add the melted butter, and blend until smooth. Set aside for 10 minutes.

Draw 2 x 2½in. (10cm) circles on each sheet of parchment paper and spoon 1 tablespoon of the mixture onto each circle. Using either the back of a spoon or an offset spatula, spread the mixture in an even layer to fill the circles. Bake 1 sheet on the middle rack of the preheated oven and the other on the shelf below for about 6–8 minutes, until the cookies are starting to turn golden at the edges.

Working quickly, remove one sheet of parchment paper from the oven at a time, leaving the other baking sheet inside and, using an offset spatula, carefully and quickly lift the cookies off the parchment paper. Flip the cookie over, lay your fortune message in the middle, and fold the cookie over it in half. Bring the points of the cookie together to make the fortune cookie curl and leave to cool in a muffin pan (this will help them to keep their shape). Repeat with the remaining cookies.

Once you have used up all of the mixture and all of your cookies are baked and shaped, slide the muffin pan into the oven for another minute to brown them evenly.

 Leave to cool in the pans before packaging in takeout boxes. Stored in an airtight container, they will keep for up to 3 days.

MAKES ABOUT 12

¾ **cup all-purpose flour**
pinch of ground ginger
pinch of salt
3 large egg whites
1 cup confectioners' (icing) sugar
1 teaspoon vanilla extract
⅔ **cup unsalted butter, melted and cooled slightly**

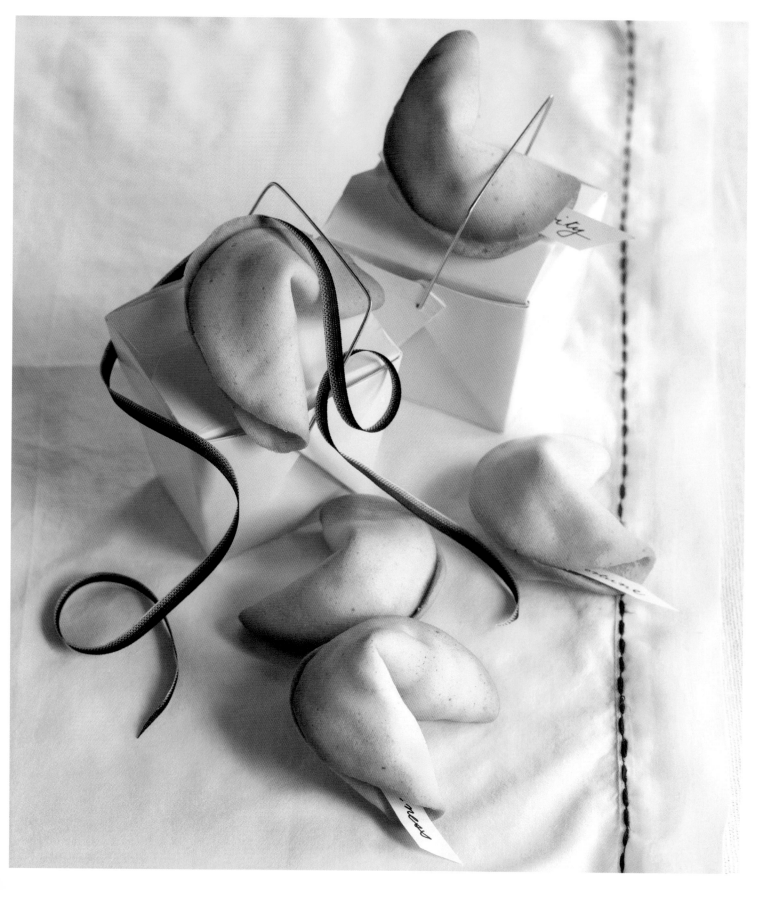

Seville Orange and Whiskey Marmalade

Seville oranges are only around for a very short season, so it makes perfect sense to make a larger batch of marmalade than you think you'll possibly need.

MAKES ABOUT 8 JARS

1¼lb Seville oranges

2 quarts (2 liters) cold water

5¼ cups granulated sugar

1¾ cups light muscovado sugar

liquid or powdered pectin (optional): use according to package instructions if set is not achieved

5 tablespoons whiskey

juice of 1 lemon

Wash the oranges thoroughly in warm water and dry them with a clean dish towel. Cut them in half and press them through a citrus press to extract as much juice as possible, but don't discard seeds, pithy membrane, or any orange flesh. Instead, tie all this up in a square of clean cheesecloth and set it aside on a saucer while you prepare the peel.

Using a sharp knife, thinly slice the peel into strips. Place in a large ceramic bowl and cover with 2 quarts (2 liters) of cold water. Add the cheesecloth bag of seeds and pith, then cover the bowl and leave the peel to soak for at least 12 hours and up to 24.

The next day, put the peel, soaking water, and cheesecloth bag into a preserving pan or other large pan. Bring to a boil, then reduce the heat, cover, and simmer extremely gently until the peel is very tender—this can take anything up to 1½ hours, depending on how thickly you have cut the peel. Don't be tempted to rush or skimp on this step, since once the sugar is added to the marmalade the peel will not soften any further. Remove the cheesecloth bag from the pan, set it aside until cool enough to handle, then squeeze it between your hands to extract every last drop of juice back into the pan. Put a couple of saucers into the fridge to be used to test the marmalade for setting point.

Add both sugars to the pan with the reserved orange and lemon juice and bring slowly to a boil to dissolve the sugar. Continue to boil steadily for about 30 minutes, skimming off any scum that rises to the surface with a slotted spoon, until setting point has been reached (see page 168). This can take up to an hour, so keep checking every 5 minutes or so.

Once setting point has been reached, add the whiskey to the pan, boil for 30 seconds, then remove from the heat. Leave the marmalade to cool in the pan for 10 minutes before spooning into sterilized jars (see page 168).

 Store for months unopened in a cool, dark cupboard or pantry. Once opened, store in the fridge. It will keep for 2–3 months.

Granola

This makes a fabulous gift to take for your host or hostess if you're invited away for the weekend. You can add any selection of dried fruit and nuts—try dried cranberries, cherries, or blueberries, or, if you prefer something more exotic, an assortment of dried tropical fruits.

Preheat the oven to 350°F (180°C).

Roughly chop the almonds and pecans and put them into a large mixing bowl. Add the oats, all the seeds, and the shredded coconut. Roughly chop the dates and apricots, add to the bowl and mix until thoroughly combined.

Heat the sunflower oil and honey in a small pan until the honey is very runny but not boiling. Pour into the oat mixture and stir to coat evenly.

Cover a large shallow roasting pan with a sheet of parchment paper, add the granola and cook in the preheated oven for 15–20 minutes. Stir the mixture regularly to ensure that the granola browns evenly. Once it is golden and starting to crisp, remove from the oven and leave to cool completely before spooning into a storage jar. Attach a label with serving instructions and ingredients.

MAKES ABOUT 4 JAM JARS

⅓ cup whole almonds
½ cup pecans
1¼ cups rolled oats
¾ cup pumpkin seeds
3 tablespoons sesame seeds
⅓ cup sunflower seeds
⅔ cup shredded coconut
4½ medjool dates, pitted
3½oz (100g) dried apricots
2 tablespoons sunflower oil
½ cup honey

 A delicious way to start the day, serve scattered over plain yogurt and with a compote of summer berries. It will keep for 2–3 weeks in an airtight container.

Chocolate Valentine's Cakes

Forget the usual chocolates and roses for Valentine's Day; instead, say "I Love You" with these chocolate heart-shaped cakes coated with dark chocolate ganache and topped with sugar paste roses. Ready-made flowers are available from specialty stores and online, but making your own roses is really very simple, just make them 24 hours before topping the cakes to allow them to dry.

You will need 6 x 4in. (10cm) heart-shaped cake pans with a depth of 1¼in. (3cm).

Preheat the oven to 350°F (180°C). Brush the insides of the pans with the melted butter and dust with 1 tablespoon of the all-purpose flour, tapping out any excess.

Melt the chopped chocolate either in a heatproof bowl set over a pan of barely simmering water, or in a microwave on a low setting. Stir until smooth and set aside to cool slightly.

Cream the butter and sugar until pale, light, and fluffy. Add the egg yolks and stir until combined. Add the cooled melted chocolate and stir again. Mix the remaining 2 tablespoons of all-purpose flour with the ground almonds, freeze-dried raspberries, if using, and salt. Add to the chocolate mixture and mix thoroughly.

In a clean bowl, whisk the egg whites until they reach stiff peaks. Stir one-quarter of the egg whites into the chocolate mixture to loosen and then, using a large metal spoon, fold in the remainder.

Line the bottom of the cake pans with parchment paper and divide the mixture between them all, then arrange on a baking sheet and bake on the middle rack of the preheated oven for 20 minutes, until risen and firm to the touch. Leave to cool in the pans for 5 minutes, then carefully run a small offset spatula around the edges and turn the cakes onto a cooling rack and leave until cold.

To make the ganache, melt together the chocolate, butter, and heavy cream either in a heatproof bowl set over a pan of barely simmering water or in a microwave on a low setting. Stir until smooth and combined. Set aside to cool and thicken slightly. Using an offset spatula, spread the ganache over the top of each cake and leave to set before decorating with sugar paste roses or fresh berries.

MAKES 6

1⅓ sticks unsalted butter, softened, plus 1 tablespoon, melted

3 tablespoons all-purpose flour

7oz (200g) plain chocolate, chopped

¾ cup superfine sugar

4 medium eggs, separated

1 cup ground almonds

2 tablespoons freeze-dried raspberries (optional)

pinch of salt

sugar paste roses, to decorate (optional)

fresh berries, to decorate (optional)

CHOCOLATE GANACHE:

7oz (200g) dark chocolate (72% cacoa solids)

⅔ stick unsalted butter

2 tablespoons heavy cream

Stored in an airtight container or cake tin, these will keep for about 4 days.

Baby Shower Cakes

Preheat the oven to 350°F (180°C). Butter an 8in (20cm) square cake pan and line the bottom with buttered parchment paper.

Cream together the softened butter and superfine sugar until light and fluffy, scraping down the sides of the bowl from time to time with a rubber spatula. Gradually add the beaten eggs (and lemon extract, if using), mixing well between additions.

Sift together the flour and baking powder with a pinch of salt and fold into the creamed mixture, followed by the milk. Fold in the ground almonds, grated lemon zest and juice, stir until smooth, then spoon into the prepared pan. Spread level and bake on the middle rack of the preheated oven for about 25 minutes, or until a skewer inserted into the middle of the cake comes out clean.

Remove from the oven and cool in the pan for 5–10 minutes before turning out onto a wire cooling rack. Once the cake is completely cold, wrap it in plastic wrap until you are ready to decorate it.

Split the cake in half horizontally using a long, serrated knife. Spread the bottom layer with the lemon curd and sandwich the layers back together. Trim the sides of the cake and cut into 9 even-sized cubes.

To make the buttercream frosting, place the egg whites in a medium-sized heatproof bowl, add the sugar, and set over a pan of barely simmering water. Whisk the mixture constantly until it is hot, thickens, turns very white and glossy and will hold a ribbon trail; this will take about 4–5 minutes. Quickly pour this meringue mixture into the bowl of an electric mixer and whisk for 2–3 minutes, until cold. Gradually add the softened butter, whisking well between additions. Add the lemon extract and stir to combine. Use the point of a toothpick to add food-coloring paste and mix until you reach the desired shade.

Pour out the grated white chocolate onto a large plate. Spread the tops and sides of each little cake with a thin layer of buttercream and spread evenly with an offset spatula, then dip the sides of each cake into the grated chocolate so that each one is completely covered. Fit a piping bag with a small, star-shaped nozzle and fill the bag with the remaining frosting. Pipe small rosettes on top of the cakes in neat rows and finish each cake with a sugar flower. Package in a single layer in a shallow box.

MAKES 9 CAKES

CAKES:

2 sticks unsalted butter, softened

1 cup superfine sugar

3 large eggs, beaten

1⅓ cups all-purpose flour

1 teaspoon lemon extract (optional)

3 level teaspoons baking powder

pinch of salt

3–4 tablespoons milk, at room temperature

⅔ cup ground almonds

grated zest and juice of ½ an organic lemon

FROSTING BUTTERCREAM:

2 tablespoons lemon curd

3 large egg whites

1 cup superfine sugar

2 sticks unsalted butter, softened

1 teaspoon lemon extract

pink, blue, yellow, and mauve food-coloring pastes

11oz (300g) white chocolate, coarsely grated

little sugar flowers to decorate

Stored in an airtight container, they will keep for 2–3 days.

Take a box of these little cakes to a baby shower or as a gift to celebrate the birth of a new baby. Tint the frosting pale pastel shades of yellow, blue, mauve, or pink, and top with little sugar flowers in contrasting colors.

Raspberry, Lemon, and Almond Friands

These little cupcakes are light as air but somehow rich at the same time and filled with almonds and fresh raspberries.

Preheat the oven to 350°F (180°C). Butter the insides of 12 friand or muffin pans and lightly dust with a little all-purpose flour, tapping out the excess.

Sift the flour, confectioners' (icing) sugar, ground almonds, and salt into a large bowl and make a well in the center. In another bowl, lightly whisk the egg whites until foamy and just holding soft peaks. Pour the egg whites and melted butter into the dry ingredients with the grated lemon zest and and, using a large metal spoon, fold the mixture together until combined.

Divide the mixture between the prepared pans, filling them three-quarters full. Drop 4 or 5 raspberries onto each cupcake and scatter the flaked almonds on top.

Bake on the middle rack of the preheated oven for about 15 minutes, until well risen and golden brown. Remove from the oven and leave to rest in the pans for 2 minutes before carefully turning out onto a wire cooling rack.

Dust lightly with confectioners' (icing) sugar before packaging.

Package in single layers in a box or vintage cake tin or individually wrap each friand in a cellophane bag. Friands are usually baked in little oval pans but you could just as easily use muffin pans or mini loaf pans. Stored in an airtight container, they will keep for about 3 days.

MAKES 10-12 FRIANDS

⅔ cup all-purpose flour, plus extra for dusting

2 cups confectioners' (icing) sugar, plus extra for dusting

1¼ cups ground almonds

pinch of salt

5 large egg whites

1¼ sticks unsalted butter, melted and cooled

grated zest of 1½ organic lemons

7oz (200g) raspberries

½ cup slivered almonds

Double Dark Chocolate, Pecan and Ginger Cookies

These are very grown-up cookies, with a double hit of chocolate and just a hint of ginger. If you prefer, you can swap the ginger for candied orange peel or dried cherries.

Break 7oz (200g) of the chocolate into pieces and melt it with the butter, either in a heatproof bowl set over a pan of barely simmering water or in the microwave on a low setting. Stir until smooth and set aside to cool slightly. Chop the remaining chocolate into chunks.

Whisk the sugar and eggs together in a large bowl for a few minutes. Add the vanilla extract, then the melted chocolate and butter mixture, and stir until smooth. Sift together the flour, baking powder, cocoa, and salt. Add to the cookie mixture with the chopped chocolate, pecans, and stem ginger and mix until thoroughly combined. Cover with plastic wrap and chill for a couple of hours, until firm.

Preheat the oven to 350°F (180°C) and line 2 baking sheets with nonstick parchment paper. Using a teaspoon, scoop balls of the cookie mixture on to the baking sheets, leaving space between them. Flatten the cookies slightly and bake in batches on the middle rack of the preheated oven for about 12 minutes, until firm but not crisp. Remove from the oven and let the cookies cool on the sheets.

Repeat with the remaining cookie dough. Cool the cookies completely before packaging.

 Stored in an airtight container, they will keep for about 5 days.

MAKES ABOUT 20 COOKIES

12oz (425g) dark chocolate

1 stick unsalted butter

1⅓ cups light muscovado or light brown sugar

3 large eggs

1 teaspoon vanilla extract

1¼ cups all-purpose flour

½ teaspoon baking powder

1 tablespoon cocoa

pinch of salt

1¼ cups pecans, chopped

1 rounded tablespoon finely chopped stem ginger

Preheat the oven to 350°F (180°C), and line the muffin pans with pretty baking cups.

Melt the chopped chocolate in a heatproof bowl, either over a pan of barely simmering water or in the microwave on a low setting. Stir until smooth and remove from the heat.

In the bowl of an electric mixer, cream together the softened butter and superfine sugar until pale, light, and fluffy. Gradually add the beaten eggs, mixing well between additions and scraping down the sides of the bowl with a rubber spatula from time to time. Add the melted chocolate and mix again until smooth.

Sift the flour, cocoa, baking powder, baking soda, and salt into a bowl. Add the dry ingredients to the creamed mixture and stir in the sour cream and boiling water. Mix until smooth, then divide between the baking cups, filling each one two-thirds full. Bake on the middle rack of the preheated oven for about 20 minutes, or until the cupcakes are well risen and a wooden skewer inserted into the middle comes out clean. Cool the cupcakes in the pan for 5 minutes, then transfer to a wire cooling rack and leave until completely cold before frosting.

To make the buttercream, pour the superfine sugar and egg whites into a medium-sized heatproof bowl and set over a pan of simmering water without allowing the bottom of the bowl to touch the water. Whisk steadily until the mixture is thick, glossy, holds a soft peak and reaches 300°F (150°C) on a sugar thermometer. Remove from the heat and scoop the mixture into the bowl of an electric mixer. Whisk for about 3–4 minutes, until cool, thick, and glossy. Gradually add the softened butter, mixing well between additions. Add the vanilla extract and mix again until smooth. Fit a large piping bag with a star-shaped nozzle and fill with the buttercream. Pipe generous swirls of frosting onto the top of each cooled cupcake.

Using your hands, break up the shredded wheat and put into a bowl. Add the melted chocolate and mix to coat thoroughly. Arrange small nests of chocolate shredded wheat on top of each cupcake, sit 4 mini eggs in each "nest," and leave to set.

Easter Nest Cupcakes

MAKES 12–16 CUPCAKES

CAKE:

3oz (75g) dark chocolate, chopped
1 stick unsalted butter, softened
1 cup superfine sugar
2 large eggs, beaten
1⅓ cups all-purpose flour
1 rounded tablespoon cocoa or malted chocolate powder (Ovaltine)
½ teaspoon baking powder
1 teaspoon baking soda
pinch of salt
½ cup sour cream, room temperature
¼ cup boiling water

MERINGUE BUTTERCREAM:

1 cup superfine sugar
3 large egg whites
2 sticks unsalted butter, softened
1 teaspoon vanilla extract

DECORATION:

2¼ cups shredded wheat
6oz (150g) dark chocolate, melted
chocolate mini eggs

Pack the cupcakes into pretty boxes. Stored in an airtight container, they will keep for about 5 days.

These little cupcakes would be perfect to take on an Easter egg hunt, packaged in individual boxes and tied with name tags. Look for pretty, pastel-colored paper baking cups and fancy little chocolate eggs to sit in the nests.

JEWISH CELEBRATION

Doughnuts

Heat the milk until warm to the touch. Add the yeast and whisk to combine, then set aside in a warm place for about 5 minutes to activate the yeast. It is ready when the milk has a thick, yeasty foam floating on top.

Pour the flour, salt, and ⅓ cup of the sugar into the bowl of a free-standing electric mixer equipped with a dough hook. Make a well in the center and add the yeasty milk, whole egg, egg yolk, and butter. Mix steadily for about 5 minutes, until the dough is smooth and elastic. It will still be slightly sticky.

Dust a work surface with a little all-purpose flour, then scrape the dough out of the mixing bowl and knead, using your hands, for 1 minute. Shape the dough into a smooth ball and place in a large, clean mixing bowl. Cover with plastic wrap and leave in a warm, draft-free place for at least 1 hour, or until the dough has doubled in size.

Lightly dust the work surface with flour again and knead the dough very gently for 1 minute. Roll it out to a thickness of ½in. Using a round cookie cutter, stamp out disks from the dough roughly 2½–3½in. (6–8cm) in diameter. Using a smaller cutter (about 1½in./4cm), stamp out a smaller disk from the middle of each doughnut.

Arrange the ring doughnuts and mini round doughnuts on a lightly floured baking sheet. Cover loosely with oiled plastic wrap and leave to rise again for 30 minutes.

Cover a large baking sheet with a triple thickness of paper towels and pour the remaining superfine sugar into a large bowl or shallow roasting pan. Pour the sunflower oil into a large, shallow pan (it should come halfway up the sides) and heat to 350–375°F (180–190°C).

Fry the doughnuts in small batches for about 1–2 minutes on each side, or until lightly browned. Remove from the oil with a slotted spoon and drain thoroughly on the paper towels before tossing in the superfine sugar. Make sure the oil comes back up to temperature before frying the next batch of doughnuts.

 These are best eaten on the day they are made.

If you have never eaten freshly cooked, homemade doughnuts then you've missed out on something utterly delicious. Doughnuts are a common Hanukkah treat, when it is traditional to eat fried foods that symbolize the miracle of the oil that was found in the temple in Jerusalem that burned for 8 nights rather than for one.

MAKES 8 RING AND 8 MINI
ROUND DOUGHNUTS

¾ **cup milk**

1½ **envelopes active dry yeast**

3¼ **cups bread flour, plus extra for dusting**

½ **teaspoon salt**

1⅔ **cups superfine sugar**

1 **whole egg, beaten**

1 **egg yolk**

⅔ **stick unsalted butter, softened**

all-purpose flour, for dusting

1 **quart sunflower oil, for deep frying**

1 **teaspoon ground cinnamon (optional)**

I have made these doughnuts into rings and mini round shapes and tossed them in superfine sugar after frying. When frying the doughnuts it is important to keep the oil at a constant temperature to ensure that they cook perfectly without either burning or absorbing too much oil.

JEWISH CELEBRATION
Lebkuchen

Lebkuchen are traditional German cookies loaded with honey and spices that are baked at Christmastime and are often elaborately decorated with royal icing. I have given a simple confectioners' (icing) sugar glaze in this recipe, but you could coat your cookies in melted dark or white chocolate instead.

MAKES ABOUT 30 COOKIES, DEPENDING ON SIZE

3 level tablespoons honey
¼ cup blackstrap molasses
½ stick unsalted butter
½ cup dark muscovado sugar
1¾ cups self-rising flour, plus extra for dusting
½ teaspoon ground cinnamon
3 teaspoons ground ginger
¼ teaspoon grated nutmeg
pinch of ground cloves
pinch of ground allspice
pinch of salt
⅔ cup ground almonds
1 tablespoon finely chopped candied peel or stem ginger
finely grated zest of ½ an orange
1 large egg, lightly beaten

GLAZE:
1½ cups confectioners' (icing) sugar
juice of ½ a lemon

Measure the honey and molasses into a small pan. Add the butter and muscovado sugar and place over low heat to melt. Stir until smooth, then remove from the heat and leave to cool.

In a large bowl, sift together the flour, spices, and salt. Add the ground almonds, the candied peel or ginger, and the grated orange zest and stir to combine. Make a well in the middle of the dry ingredients and add the melted butter and honey mixture and the beaten egg. Mix well with a wooden spoon or spatula until smooth. Cover with plastic wrap and chill for around 4 hours, or until firm.

Preheat the oven to 350°F (180°C) and cover 2 baking sheets with nonstick parchment paper. Lightly dust a work surface with a little all-purpose flour and roll out the cookie dough to a thickness of just under ½in. (1cm). Using cookie cutters, stamp out shapes and arrange on the prepared baking sheets. Bake on the middle rack of the preheated oven for around 15 minutes, or until firm and just starting to brown at the edges.

While the cookies are baking, prepare the glaze. Sift the confectioners' (icing) sugar into a bowl and add a dash of lemon juice and enough hot water to make a smooth glaze.

Remove the cookies from the oven and brush with a little of the glaze while still warm. Cool on wire racks before packaging.

 Stored in an airtight container, they will keep for up to 1 week.

JEWISH CELEBRATION
Rugelach

Rugelach are little crescents of tender, flakey, buttery dough not dissimilar to croissants. They are eaten throughout the year, but are often made for Hannukah. In this recipe, the rugelach are filled with dark chocolate and chopped pecans, but they are just as delicious with dried fruit and nuts.

In a mixing bowl, beat together the butter and cream cheese until smooth. Add the superfine sugar and vanilla extract and mix again. Sift the all-purpose flour and salt, add to the bowl, and mix until smooth and thoroughly combined. Turn the dough out onto a floured work surface and divide into 4 even pieces. Flatten each one into a disk, wrap in plastic wrap, and chill for a few hours, or until firm.

Preheat the oven to 350°F (180°C) and line 2 baking sheets with nonstick parchment paper.

To make the filling, finely chop the chocolate and pecans and mix with the ground cinnamon and superfine sugar.

Lightly dust a work surface with a little all-purpose flour and roll each pastry disk out into a neat circle about the thickness of a dime. Spread with an even layer of jam and scatter the chocolate pecan mixture over the top. Using a long knife or a pizza wheel, divide each circle into 6 triangles. Roll each triangle into a crescent, starting from the outside and rolling toward the point.

Arrange the pastries on the prepared baking sheets, brush with a little beaten egg, and sprinkle with superfine sugar. Bake 1 sheet at a time on the middle rack of the preheated oven for around 20 minutes, until golden.

 Stored in an airtight container, they will keep for about 3 days.

MAKES 24 PASTRIES

DOUGH:

2 sticks unsalted butter, softened

1 cup cream cheese

⅓ cup superfine sugar

1 teaspoon vanilla extract

2 cups all-purpose flour, plus extra for rolling

pinch of salt

FILLING:

3½oz (100g) dark chocolate

1 cup toasted pecans

2 teaspoons ground cinnamon

⅓ cup superfine sugar

¼ cup cherry, apricot, or raspberry jam

TOPPING:

1 egg, beaten

superfine sugar, for sprinkling

CHRISTMAS

Stained Glass Snowflake Cookies

I have used festive snowflake cutters for these cookies, but the same idea works just as well for almost any shape. They look beautiful hanging at a window, allowing the light to shine through the "stained glass." Or you can give one cookie to each guest as a place setting or table gift at the Christmas dinner table.

You will need a selection of snowflake cookie cutters.

Cream the softened butter and confectioners' (icing) sugar together until pale and light. Add the whole egg and vanilla extract and mix again until thoroughly combined. Sift the flour with the salt, add to the bowl, and mix again until smooth.

Gather the dough into a ball, flatten into a disk, and wrap in plastic wrap. Chill for a couple of hours, or until firm.

Meanwhile divide the boiled candies into separate colors, place in freezer bags, and crush using a rolling pin.

Preheat the oven to 350°F (180°C) and line 2 baking sheets with nonstick parchment paper.

Lightly dust a work surface with flour and roll out the dough until it is about the thickness of a quarter. Using the snowflake cutters, stamp out snowflakes in assorted sizes and arrange on the prepared baking sheets. Carefully and neatly fill the holes in the snowflakes with the crushed, boiled candies. Bake in batches on the middle rack of the preheated oven for about 12 minutes, until the cookies are pale golden and the boiled candies have melted and filled the holes.

Cool the cookies on the trays until hardened, and package into boxes lined with baking parchment or waxed paper once completely cold.

 These will keep for 4–5 days in an airtight container.

MAKES 8–12 COOKIES

2 sticks unsalted butter, softened

1¼ cups confectioners' (icing) sugar

1 large egg, beaten

1 teaspoon vanilla extract

2¾ cups all-purpose flour, plus extra for rolling

pinch of salt

assorted flavored and colored candies

Date and Ginger Cake

Here's a light, gingery, fruit-filled Christmas cake that is cut into smaller cakes and then decorated to look like mini gifts. If you like, you can simply cover the top of each small cake with a layer of marzipan and royal icing. Stamp out icing stars to decorate and embellish with silver sugar balls or edible glitter. To finish, tie each little cake in a festive ribbon and add a gift tag.

Prepare the dry ingredients the day before you plan to bake the cake. Chop the dates into pieces roughly the same size as a raisin and finely chop the stem ginger. Mix the dates, stem ginger, golden raisins, and raisins in a large bowl with the grated lemon and orange zests and juices. Add the ginger wine, stir well, cover with plastic wrap and set aside to soak and absorb the liquid overnight.

Preheat the oven to 300°F (150°C) and position the shelf just below the middle of the oven. Butter a 9in. (23cm) cake pan and line the bottom and sides with a double thickness of parchment paper.

Sift the flour, baking powder, ground ginger, and mixed spice together on to a sheet of parchment paper and add the ground almonds.

In a large bowl or a free-standing mixer, cream the softened butter and both sugars together until light. Gradually add the beaten eggs, mixing well between additions. If the mixture appears curdled at any stage, add a tablespoon of the sifted flour mixture and continue to add the egg until it has all been incorporated.

Continued on next page

MAKES 1 X 9in (23cm) SQUARE
OR 9 INDIVIDUAL CAKES

CAKE:

7oz (200g) pitted dates

4 pieces of stem ginger in syrup

1 packed cup golden raisins

1 packed cup raisins

grated zest and juice of 1 organic lemon

grated zest and juice of 1 orange

5 tablespoons ginger wine

1¼ cups all-purpose flour

2½ teaspoons baking powder

3 teaspoons ground ginger

2 teaspoons pumpkin pie spice

1 cup ground almonds

2¼ sticks unsalted butter, softened

1 cup light muscovado sugar

1 cup dark muscovado sugar

3 large eggs, beaten

3 tablespoons milk

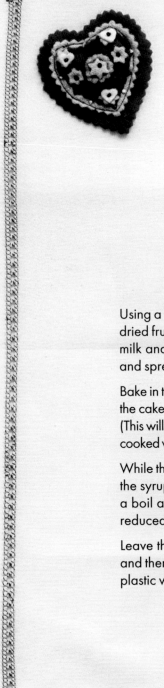

LEMON AND GINGER SYRUP:

3 tablespoons ginger syrup, from the stem ginger jar

2 tablespoons demerara or light brown sugar

juice of ½ a lemon

juice of ½ an orange

5 tablespoons brandy or ginger wine

Using a large metal spoon or spatula, fold the sifted dry ingredients and dried fruits into the cake mix and stir until thoroughly combined. Add the milk and mix again. Spoon the cake mixture into the prepared pan(s) and spread level with the back of a spoon.

Bake in the preheated oven for about 1½ hours, loosely covering the top of the cake with a sheet of parchment paper halfway though the baking time. (This will prevent the top of the cake from browning too quickly.) The cake is cooked when a skewer inserted into the middle comes out with a moist crumb.

While the cake is cooking, prepare the lemon and ginger syrup. Place all the syrup ingredients in a small pan and set over medium heat. Bring to a boil and stir to dissolve the sugar. Simmer for about 5 minutes, until reduced by one-third. Remove from the heat and leave to cool.

Leave the cake to cool in the pan on a wire rack for about 20 minutes and then turn out onto the rack and leave until completely cold. Wrap in plastic wrap until ready to ice and decorate.

TO ICE THE CAKE:

⅓ **cup apricot jam**

**confectioners' (icing) sugar,
for dusting**

18oz (500g) natural marzipan

1¾lb (850g) ready-to-roll royal icing

red food coloring paste

small silver sugar balls

ribbon

Using a large knife, trim the edges of the cake and cut into 9 even-sized cubes. Melt the jam in a small pan with a tablespoon of water. Sift to remove any lumps and brush the jam in an even layer over the top of each cake.

Divide the marzipan into 9 even-sized pieces. Dust a clean work surface with a little confectioners' (icing) sugar and roll each piece of marzipan out into a square, about ⅛in (2–3mm) thick. Carefully lay one square over a jam-covered cake and use your hands to smooth it evenly over the top and sides. Trim off any excess and repeat with the other cakes.

Cut off one quarter of the ready-made icing and tint it red using the food coloring paste. Cover with plastic wrap and set aside.

Divide the white icing into 10 even-sized pieces. Lightly dust a clean work surface with confectioners' (icing) sugar and roll 1 piece of icing out to a thickness of a dime. Lightly brush one of the marzipan-covered cakes with cooled, boiled water. Carefully lay the icing over the top of the cake so that it drapes over the sides. Use your hands to smooth the icing so that it covers the cake evenly. Trim off any excess and repeat with the remaining cakes.

Roll the remaining white and red icing out and cut into thin strips using a pasta wheel or large knife. Arrange the strips as ribbons over each cake and twist shorter lengths into bows. Lightly brush with a little water and use to decorate the top of the cake.

 Package each cake into a festive box. Stored in an airtight container, these cakes will keep for up to 2 weeks.

CHRISTMAS

Panettone

Brush the inside of an 8in, deep-sided cake pan with sunflower oil. Place the raisins into a small bowl, cover with boiling water, and set aside for 20 minutes to plump up. Drain the raisins and dry on paper towels. Mix them with the candied peel and the lemon and orange zest.

Heat the milk until it is warm to the touch and add the active dry yeast and 1 teaspoon of the superfine sugar. Mix well and leave to one side for 5 minutes to allow the yeast to activate and form a thick foam on top of the milk.

Place 2 cups of the flour, the remaining superfine sugar, and the salt into the bowl of an electric mixer equipped with a dough hook. Make a well in the middle of the dry ingredients and add the warm milk and yeast mixture, whole egg and yolk, honey, vanilla extract, and softened butter. Mix for about 5 minutes, until the dough is smooth, soft, slightly sticky, and elastic. You may need to add a little more flour if the dough is too sticky.

Add the dried fruit and grated zests and mix again until well distributed throughout the dough. Turn the dough out onto a work surface, lightly dust with flour, and knead for 1 minute. Shape the dough into a smooth ball and place in a large, clean bowl. Cover with plastic wrap and leave in a warm, draft-free place for at least 2 hours, or until doubled in size.

Lightly dust the work surface with a little more flour and lightly knead the dough again for 1 minute. Shape into a ball and place in the prepared pan, smooth side uppermost. Loosely cover with oiled plastic wrap and leave for at least 2–4 hours, until the dough is well risen and has at least doubled in size again. (This will take considerably longer if your kitchen is on the cool side.)

Preheat the oven to 325°F (170°C). To make the egg wash, beat the egg yolk and milk together and gently brush over the top of the panettone. Using a long sharp knife, cut a cross into the top of the loaf and leave to rise for another 10–15 minutes.

Bake the panettone in the bottom third of the preheated oven for about 45 minutes, or until well risen and golden brown. If the top is browning too quickly, turn the oven down slightly for the last 15 minutes of baking.

Leave the panettone to cool in the pan for 5 minutes before turning out onto a wire cooling rack.

 Wrapped and stored in an airtight container, it will keep for 1 week.

SERVES 8–10

sunflower oil, for brushing pan
½ cup raisins
2oz candied peel, finely chopped
grated zest of 1 organic lemon
grated zest of 1 orange
½ cup milk
1 level tablespoon active dry yeast
¼ cup superfine sugar
3¼ cups bread flour, plus extra for dusting
½ teaspoon salt
1 large egg, beaten
1 large egg yolk, beaten
1 tablespoon honey
2 teaspoons vanilla extract
⅔ stick unsalted butter, softened

EGG WASH:

1 egg yolk
1 tablespoon milk or cream

This sweet, fruity bread is traditionally eaten in Italy at Christmas, and is delicious cut into thick slices and served for breakfast with a steaming cup of coffee. Any leftovers can be turned into a very special and indulgent bread and butter pudding. Present the whole loaf wrapped in a large sheet of cellophane and tied with a big gauzy ribbon.

CHRISTMAS
Stollen

Stollen is a Christmas spiced bread originating in Germany that's loaded with dried fruits and filled with a thick layer of marzipan. At this time of year, with numerous gifts to think about, it makes perfect sense to double up on your baking, especially as you'll never be short of worthy recipients.

Place the raisins, golden raisins, currants, peel and cherries in a medium-sized bowl. Add the clementine or orange zest and juice and the brandy and leave to soak for an hour or so until the fruit has absorbed almost all of the liquid. Add the chopped almonds and mix well.

Sift the flour, salt, mixed spice, ground cardamom, and superfine sugar into the bowl of a free-standing electric mixer equipped with a dough hook. Warm the milk, add the active dry yeast and stir well. Set aside, until the yeast has formed a thick foam on top of the milk (5–10 minutes), then add to the dry ingredients with the softened butter, vanilla, and the beaten egg. Knead the dough in the mixer for about 5 minutes, until smooth. Add the soaked fruit and nuts and mix again, until evenly distributed throughout the dough.

Turn the dough out onto a lightly floured work surface and shape into a ball. Place in a large, clean bowl, cover with plastic wrap and leave in a warm, draft-free place for at least 1 hour, or until doubled in size.

Turn the dough out onto a lightly floured work surface again and knead lightly for 1 minute. Divide into three even pieces and roll each piece out to the size of a rectange, roughly 8 x 6in. (20 x 5cm). Divide the marzipan into 3 even pieces and roll each one into a log 6in. (15cm) long. Place a marzipan log just off the middle of each piece of dough, brush the edges with a little milk, then fold the dough over the marzipan and press to seal.

Arrange the stollen on nonstick baking sheets, cover loosely with lightly oiled clingfilm and leave in a warm, draft-free place until doubled in size. Preheat the oven to 350°F (180°C).

Bake the stollen, one at a time, on the middle rack of the preheated oven for about 25 minutes, or until risen and golden brown. Cool on wire racks, then dust liberally with confectioners' (icing) sugar before packaging into cellophane packages tied with festive ribbon.

 Stollen will keep for a week or so if wrapped well in foil or in a tin and is delicious warmed and sliced for breakfast.

MAKES 3 LOAVES

½ **packed cup raisins**

½ **packed cup golden raisins**

3 **tablespoons currants**

2oz (50g) **candied peel, finely chopped**

2oz (50g) **natural candied cherries, quartered**

grated zest and juice of 2 **clementines or** 1 **orange**

2 **tablespoons brandy**

½ **cup blanched almonds, roughly chopped**

4 **cups bread flour, plus extra for rolling**

½ **teaspoon salt**

1 **teaspoon pumpkin pie spice**

seeds from 5 **cardamom pods, ground**

¼ **cup superfine sugar**

1 **cup milk**

2 **envelopes active dry yeast**

1 **stick unsalted butter, softened**

1 **teaspoon vanilla extract**

1 **large egg, beaten**

1lb (450g) **marzipan**

confectioners' (icing) sugar, for dusting

Chocolate, Nut, and Fig Cake

This cake makes a fantastic, indulgent alternative to the more traditional Christmas cake and is perfect served in small slices at a large festive gathering.

Finely chop the figs and place them in a bowl with the brandy or Marsala. Leave to soak for a couple of hours.

Preheat the oven to 300°F (150°C) and position a rack just below the middle of the oven. Butter a 9in. (23cm) springform cake pan and line the bottom with a disk of buttered parchment paper.

Toast the hazelnuts and almonds in the preheated oven for about 7 minutes, until pale gold in color. Cool completely, then finely chop, either in the food processor or by hand. Add the flour, cinnamon, and salt and mix to combine thoroughly.

Place the chocolate in a heatproof bowl with the diced butter. Melt the chocolate and butter either over a pan of barely simmering water, without allowing the bottom of the bowl to touch the water, or in the microwave on a low setting. Stir until smooth, then set aside to cool slightly.

Whisk together the egg yolks, superfine sugar and honey until the mixture is thick, pale, and will hold a ribbon trail—this is easiest in a free-standing electric mixer equipped with a whisk attachment. Add the melted chocolate mixture, the flour and nut mixture, and the soaked figs and any leftover brandy and stir until smooth.

In a spotlessly clean and dry bowl, whisk the egg whites with a pinch of salt until stiff but not dry. Stir a large spoonful of the egg whites into the cake mixture to loosen it slightly, then gently fold in the remainder.

MAKES 1 X 9in (23cm) ROUND CAKE

CAKE:

4½oz (125g) ready-to-eat dried figs

3 tablespoons brandy or Marsala

1 cup blanched hazelnuts

1 cup blanched almonds

⅓ cup all-purpose flour

½ teaspoon ground cinnamon

pinch of salt

12oz (350g) dark chocolate (72% cacoa solids), broken up

1⅓ sticks unsalted butter, diced

5 large eggs, separated

⅓ cup superfine sugar

¼ cup honey

3–4 tablespoons apricot jam

confectioners' (icing) sugar, for dusting

7oz (200g) natural marzipan

7oz (200g) dark chocolate (72% cacoa solids)

⅔ stick unsalted butter

2 tablespoons heavy cream

1 tablespoon honey

Spoon the mixture into the prepared pan and spread level. Bake on the middle rack of the preheated oven for about 1 hour, or until a skewer inserted into the middle of the cake comes out with a moist crumb. Loosely cover the cake with a sheet of parchment paper for the last 15 minutes of cooking time if the top appears to be browning too quickly. Cool the cake in the pan for 20 minutes, then turn out onto a wire rack and leave until completely cold. Wrapped well in foil, the cake will keep for 2 weeks if you do not want to ice it right away.

Once the cake is cold (or the next day), it can be iced. Place the cake on a cooling rack set over a baking sheet. Melt the apricot jam over low heat or in a microwave, and pass it through a sifter. Brush the top and sides of the cake with a thin layer of the melted jam. Lightly dust a clean work surface or board with a little confectioners' (icing) sugar and roll the marzipan out into a large thin circle about 12in. (30cm) in diameter. Carefully lay the marzipan over the cake to cover the top and sides completely in a smooth, thin layer. Trim off any excess. Brush with a little more warm jam.

Melt together the chocolate, butter, cream, and honey. Stir until smooth, then remove from the heat. Set aside for about 20 minutes to cool and thicken slightly. Pour the icing on to the top of the cake and smooth it over the sides to coat evenly, using an offset spatula. Leave the cake in a cool place to allow the icing to set before serving in thin slices.

Package into a large container or cake tin and, once opened, keep well wrapped.

Un-iced, the cake will keep well for a couple of weeks if wrapped in parchment paper and plastic wrap. Once iced, stored in an airtight container, the cake will keep for about 1 week.

CHRISTMAS

Panforte

Chock full of nuts, dried fruit, and spices—panforte is delicious dusted with confectioners' (icing) sugar, cut into small wedges or squares, and served after dinner with coffee. Originally from Sienna, Italy, and, although not specifically a festive treat, it certainly makes an ideal Christmas present. I have suggested baking two smaller cakes so that you can make two gifts at once.

Grease 2 x 8in. (18cm) round cake pans and line the bottom of each with a disk of rice paper.

Preheat the oven to 350°F (180°C). Spread the almonds and hazelnuts on a baking sheet and toast in the preheated oven for about 5–7 minutes, until lightly golden. Cool slightly, then roughly chop with the pistachios and place in a large bowl. Add the chopped dried fruit and mix well. In another small bowl, mix together the spices, flour, cocoa, and salt. Add to the dried fruit and nuts and mix until thoroughly combined. Lower the oven temperature to 300°F (150°C).

Combine the honey and sugar in a medium-sized pan and stir over low heat until the sugar has dissolved. Bring to a boil and continue to cook until the mixture reaches 240°F (115°C) on a candy thermometer. Remove from the heat, pour into the fruit and nut mixture, and mix well. Spoon into the prepared pan and spread level.

Bake on the middle rack of the preheated oven for 45–60 minutes, until firm. Remove from the oven and cool in the pan. Run an offset spatula around the edge of the pan and carefully ease out the panforte. Dust with confectioners' (icing) sugar to serve.

 Stored in an airtight container, panforte will keep for weeks.

MAKES 2 CAKES

sunflower oil, for greasing

1 cup blanched almonds

1 cup blanched hazelnuts

¾ cup unsalted shelled pistachios

2 cups mixed dried fruits, including apricots, candied peel, raisins, figs, and medjool dates, roughly chopped

1 teaspoon ground cinnamon

½ teaspoon ground ginger

½ teaspoon ground cloves

½ teaspoon ground nutmeg

½ teaspoon freshly ground black pepper

¾ cup all-purpose flour

1 rounded tablespoon cocoa

pinch of salt

½ cup honey

1 cup superfine sugar

confectioners' (icing) sugar, to serve

Cashew and Almond Barfi

This is my version of a popular Indian sweet that is often prepared and given during festivals and holidays. Edible silver leaf is readily available from online suppliers, and is usually sold in books of 12 or 25 small sheets.

Line a 8in. (20cm) square baking pan with lightly oiled parchment paper.

Put the cashews into a food processor and blend until finely ground. Add the ground almonds and pulse for another 30 seconds. Mix with the superfine sugar, condensed milk, milk, ground cardamom, and rosewater.

Heat the clarified butter or ghee in a large nonstick frying pan and add the nut mixture. Stir constantly over low heat for about 10–15 minutes, until the mixture thickens and comes away from the pan smoothly in a thick mass. It should be the consistency of a loose bread dough or choux pastry. Pour the mixture into the prepared pan and spread level with an offset spatula. Leave to cool for 10 minutes.

Very carefully peel one sheet of silver leaf at a time from the book and lay on the surface of the barfi to cover it completely. Leave to set completely, then cut into diamonds with a sharp knife or a pizza wheel.

Package in a single layer in a shallow box lined with waxed or nonstick parchment paper.

 Stored in an airtight container, these will keep for up to 1 week.

MAKES 20–24 PIECES

¾ **cup unsalted cashews**

¾ **cup ground almonds**

⅔ **cup superfine sugar**

14oz (300ml) can condensed milk

¼ **cup milk**

½ **teaspoon ground cardamom**

1 **teaspoon rosewater**

2 **tablespoons clarified butter or ghee**

6 **sheets of edible silver leaf**

Wedding Cake

Making a wedding cake for someone special is perhaps the ultimate food gift. I've lost count of the number of wedding cakes that I've made for friends and family, ranging from mountains of cupcakes to variations on this particular chocolate cake.

You will need to make this cake one layer at a time.

To make the smaller cake: preheat the oven to 325°F (170°C) and line the base and sides of the 8in square pan (2½–3in./7–8cm deep) with a double thickness of buttered parchment paper.

Break the chocolate into chunks and place in a medium-sized heatproof bowl. Add the diced butter and melt either over a pan of barely simmering water or in a microwave on a low setting. Stir until smooth, then remove from the heat and cool slightly.

Pour the egg yolks and superfine sugar into the bowl of a free-standing electric mixer and whisk until pale and doubled in volume, scraping down the sides of the bowl with a rubber spatula from time to time. Add the cooled chocolate and butter mixture and the coffee extract and stir until smooth. Fold in the ground almonds and flour, using a large metal spoon.

In another large bowl, whisk the egg whites with the salt until they hold stiff peaks. Stir one-third of the egg whites into the chocolate mixture to loosen it slightly, then fold in the remainder using a large metal spoon. Carefully pour the mixture into the prepared pan, spread level and bake just below the middle of the preheated oven for 1 hour and 20 minutes, or until a wooden skewer inserted into the middle of the cake comes out clean. Remove from the oven and cool the cake in the pan.

Continued on next page

MAKES 1 CAKE
(SERVES ABOUT 50 GUESTS)

SMALLER CAKE:

10oz (300g) dark chocolate

1¾ sticks unsalted butter, diced

6 large eggs, separated

1 cup superfine sugar

1 teaspoon coffee extract

1½ cups ground almonds

1 rounded tablespoon all-purpose flour

pinch of salt

LARGER CAKE:

1¼lb dark chocolate

3½ sticks unsalted butter, diced

12 large eggs, separated

2 cups superfine sugar

2 teaspoons coffee extract

3¼ cups ground almonds

2 rounded tablespoons all-purpose flour

pinch of salt

TO FINISH:

½ cup apricot jam

18oz (500g) dark chocolate

CHOCOLATE GANACHE:

1¼lb (600g) dark chocolate (72% cacoa solids)

2¼ sticks unsalted butter, diced

⅓ cup heavy cream

YOU WILL NEED:

1 x 8in. (20cm) square cake pan

1 x 10in. (25cm) square cake pan

1 x 8in. (20cm) cake plate

1 x 10in. (25cm) cake plate

dowel rods

To make the larger cake: butter and line the bottom and sides of the 10in. (25cm) square cake pan with a double thickness of buttered parchment paper. Follow the method above, but use the larger quantities and cook the cake in the bottom half of the oven for about 2 hours, or until a wooden skewer inserted into the middle of the cake comes out clean. Remove from the oven and cool the cake in the pan.

When the cakes are completely cold, wrap them in plastic wrap until you are ready to ice them.

When you are ready to ice the cakes, place them on the cake plates right side uppermost. Melt the apricot jam with a splash of water in a small pan and pass though a sifter to remove any lumps. Brush the top and sides of the cakes with an even coating of jam.

To make the ganache: break the chocolate into pieces and place in a heatproof bowl with the diced butter and heavy cream. Set the bowl over a pan of barely simmering water and stir until melted and smooth. Remove from the heat and stir the ganache well to ensure that the ingredients are thoroughly combined. Leave to cool and thicken slightly.

Cover the top and sides of each cake with the ganache, spreading it smoothly and evenly with a palette knife.

Melt the remaining chocolate and spread it in a thin, even layer over 2–3 large sheets of nonstick parchment paper. Leave in a cool place until set and then, using a large knife, cut it into strips about 1in. (2cm) wide and just a little higher than the sides of the cakes. Using a palette knife, carefully lift the chocolate strips off the paper and press on to the sides of the cakes, overlapping each strip slightly.

When you are ready to assemble the cakes, you will first need to push some dowel rods into the bottom layer to ensure that it will support the weight of the top cake. Push one dowel rod into the bottom cake, right down to the cake plate, and mark the height of the cake. Cut about 8 pieces of dowel the same length and push these into the cake, spacing them evenly apart. Place the large cake on the cake stand and carefully position the smaller cake on top. Decorate the cakes with a variety of small roses in your choice of colors.

 The cake bases can be baked in advance and frozen un-iced, or will keep well for 3–4 days un-iced and wrapped well in plastic wrap.

Small roses in varying sizes and shades make the most beautiful decoration and can be matched to the bridal flowers and color scheme.

Beet-cured Gravadlax

Peel the beets and coarsely grate into a large bowl. Lightly crush the peppercorns, fennel seeds, and juniper berries in a mortar and pestle and add to the beet. Add the salt, sugar, lemon zest, and 2 tablespoons of the chopped dill and mix well.

Cover a large, shallow roasting pan with a triple thickness of large sheets of plastic wrap. Scatter one-third of the beet mixture on to the middle of the plastic wrap and lay the salmon fillet on top, skin-side down. Cover the salmon with the remaining beet mixture and drizzle the vodka over the top. Wrap the salmon tightly in plastic wrap, cover with another baking sheet, and weigh down with a couple of cans of tomatoes, or something similar. Leave the salmon to cure in the fridge for 2 days.

Before you package and serve the salmon, scrape off as much salt as possible from the fish and pat it dry with paper towels. Scatter the remaining 2 tablespoons of chopped dill over the top. Thinly slice the gravad lax, then wrap in waxed or greaseproof paper and serve with pickled cucumber slices and rye bread.

 Well-wrapped in the fridge, this will keep for 4–5 days.

The salmon in this recipe is cured rather than cooked, so it pays to use the very best fish that you can find. Gravad lax makes a perfect starter to a New Year's Eve party (or any celebratory dinner), or it could be served the next day when perhaps spending hours in the kitchen is not high on the agenda. Serve with the Pickled Cucumbers and a rustic loaf of rye or soda bread.

SERVES 8

3 medium-sized raw beets
2 teaspoons black peppercorns
2 teaspoons fennel seeds
4 juniper berries
⅓ cup coarse sea salt
⅓ cup golden granulated sugar
grated zest of 1 organic lemon
¼ cup chopped dill
2¾lb (1.25kg) salmon fillet, scaled and pin bones removed
¼ cup vodka

Pickled Cucumbers

Thinly slice the cucumber and place in a colander. Scatter the salt over the top and mix well. Leave for 1 hour, to allow any excess moisture to drain from the cucumber.

Rinse the cucumber slices under cold running water, then pat dry on paper towels, and place in a bowl. Whisk the remaining ingredients together, pour over the cucumber, and mix well. Season with freshly ground black pepper and serve.

 It will keep for 4 days in the fridge.

1 cucumber
2 teaspoons salt
2 rounded tablespoons chopped dill
2 teaspoons superfine sugar
2 tablespoons white wine vinegar
1 tablespoon olive oil
2 teaspoons yellow mustard seeds
freshly ground black pepper

Brinjal Pickle

Serve this pickle with any Indian meal and alongside Mango Chutney (page 106) and a stack of poppadums. It's equally delicious served with any cold roasted meats.

Trim the eggplants and cut into 1 in. (2cm) cubes. Place in a colander and sprinkle with the salt. Set the colander over a bowl and leave the eggplants to degorge (release their bitter juices) for at least 1 hour.

Place the cumin, coriander, fenugreek, and fennel seeds in a dry frying pan and toast over medium heat. When the seeds start to give off a lovely, toasty aroma and are just starting to brown, remove from the heat and finely grind using a mortar and pestle. Add the cinnamon stick, mustard seeds, and turmeric and set aside.

Rinse the eggplant cubes quickly under cold water and pat dry on paper towels. Heat 2 tablespoons of the sunflower oil in a large sauté pan over medium to high heat. Add one-third of the eggplants and fry until soft and starting to brown. Transfer from the pan to a bowl, and cook the remaining eggplants in batches in the same way.

Heat the remaining 2 tablespoons of sunflower oil in the pan and add the onions, garlic, ginger, chili peppers, and red peppers. Cook over medium heat for about 7–8 minutes, until soft and just starting to color. Add all the spices and continue to cook for another couple of minutes. Return the eggplants to the pan along with the tamarind paste, vinegar, and sugar. Bring to a boil, then reduce the heat to a very gentle simmer, and continue to cook for another 30 minutes, until the pickle has thickened and the vegetables are very tender.

Taste the pickle and add fresh lime juice and more salt, if needed. Spoon into sterilized jars (see page 168) and seal immediately. Once the pickle is completely cold, label the jars and store in a cool, dry place for at least 1 month before opening.

Store, unopened, for months in a dark, cool cupboard or pantry. Once opened and stored in the fridge, it will keep for at least 2–3 months.

MAKES 3–4 X 1lb (450g) JARS

4 medium eggplants
2 tablespoons salt
2 teaspoons cumin seeds
2 teaspoons coriander seeds
1 teaspoon fenugreek seeds
1 teaspoon fennel seeds
1 cinnamon stick
2 teaspoons black or brown mustard seeds
2 teaspoons ground turmeric
½ cup sunflower oil
1 onion, finely chopped
2 fat garlic cloves, crushed
1½ in. (4cm) piece of fresh ginger
2 long red or green chili peppers, seeded and finely chopped
2 red peppers, seeded and diced
1 rounded tablespoon tamarind paste
1 cup white malt vinegar or white wine vinegar
5 rounded tablespoons light brown sugar
juice of 1 lime

Hot Chili Pepper Vodka for Bloody Mary

If you like a Bloody Mary with a kick to it, then adding a measure of this fiery chili pepper-infused vodka is certainly one way to make it just so. You can make this as hot as you like and infuse the vodka with a selection of chili peppers to suit your taste. Once the chili peppers have been strained off, the vodka can be stored in the freezer and served ice cold in shot glasses if you're brave.

MAKES 1 BOTTLE

6 medium-sized fresh chili peppers, red and green

25fl oz (750ml) bottle premium vodka

2 sheets edible silver or gold leaf, optional

Cut the chili peppers in half and remove the seeds. Pour the vodka into a Mason jar, add the chili peppers and cover with a tight-fitting lid. Shake the vodka and leave in a cool, dry place for at least one week to allow the chili peppers to infuse the vodka.

Taste the vodka after one week and, if it's fiery enough, strain off the chili peppers and decant the vodka into a clean bottle. If the vodka is not spicy enough, leave it for another week. This will depend entirely on the strength of your chili peppers, which can vary enormously.

To make your vodka that little bit extra-special, give it some sparkle with edible silver or gold leaf. Take about one cupful of the chili pepper vodka and pour into a blender. Add two or three sheets of silver leaf and pulse until the silver is finely chopped. Pour back into the remaining vodka, seal the bottle, and label.

 Stored in the fridge, this will keep for months.

Setting Point

To test if your jam or jelly has reached setting point, drop a teaspoonful onto a cold saucer. Leave for 1 minute, then push the jam or jelly with the tip of your finger. If it wrinkles, it's ready to pour into jars. If not, continue to cook and test every couple of minutes.

Sterilizing

It's important to sterilize the jars and bottles that you use for storing your food gifts, since the contents will keep for far longer that way (any dirt contaminates the food inside, causing it to spoil quickly).

Sterilizing is quick and easy and can be done in the oven or in the dishwasher.

Heat the oven to 350°F (180°C)—don't be tempted to heat the oven any higher or you may risk breaking the glass. Lay a double layer of newspaper on each oven shelf (no need to cover the floor) and arrange the jars on top, making sure the jars are not touching. Close the oven door and heat the jars for about 20 minutes. Using thick oven mitts, remove each jar from the oven and place on a heatproof mat. Do NOT add cold food to hot jars.

Alternatively, wash clean jars in your dishwasher and, when they are ready, add hot food to the hot jars, or wait for them to cool down.

Recipes for occasions

Mother's Day

Shortbreads
Brownies
Herbal teas
Macaroons
Madeleines
Nougat
Marshmallows
Raspberry or strawberry pastilles
Raspberry and rose wafers
Raspberry, lemon, and almond friands
Turkish delight

Father's Day

Barbecue sauce
Brinjal chutney
Cheese sablés
Cherry tomato and sweet chilli jam
Coffee and cardamon toffee
Dark chocolate and ginger cookies
Hot chili pepper jelly
Mango chutney
Oatmeal biscuits for cheee
Pickled shallots
Sea-salted caramels
Seville orange marmalade

Valentine's Day

Chocolate truffles
Chocolate Valentine's cakes
Fortune cookies
Lollipops
Love heart sugar cubes
Marshmallows
Raspberry and rose wafers

Easter

Easter cupcakes
Greek honey cookies

Housewarming

Biscotti
Cherry jam
Chocolate and hazlenut spread
Doughnuts
Duck confit
Fennel seed, chili pepper, and
parmesan grissini
Glogg
Granola
Hot chili pepper vodka
Lemon and passion fruit curd
Limoncello
Mango chutney
Tortellini with roasted butternut
squash, spinach, and ricotta

Baby Shower

Baby cakes
Love heart sugar cubes
Macaroons
Marshmallows
Raspberry, lemon, and almond friands
Strawberry and rose cordial

Birthday

Baby cakes
Chocolate nut and fig cake
Madeleines
Turkish delight

Bachelorette Party

Fortune cookies
Limoncello
Lollipops
Love heart sugar cubes
Macaroons
Marshmallows
Raspberry and rose wafers
Summer berry vodka
Rhubarb and vanilla vodka

New Year's Day

Cheese sablés
Chocolate nut and fig cake
Fortune cookies
Glogg
Hot chili pepper vodka
Oatmeal crackers for cheese
Panforte
Picallili
Pork rillettes
Spiced nuts
Vin d'oranges

House Guest

Cordials
Candied peels
Chocolate coated candied almonds
Chocolate truffles
Creamy vanilla fudge
Damson cheese
Granola
Macaroons
Nougat
Seville orange marmalade
Strawberry and vanilla conserve

Christmas

Candied peels
Duck confit
Glogg
Lebkuchen
Nougat
Panettone
Panforte
Pecan snowball cookies
Stained glass cookies
Spiced cranberry jelly
Spiced nuts
Stollen

Index

Index

Acknowledgments

I would like to say a huge thank you to all the fabulous people who were involved in the creation of this book. To everyone at Kyle Cathie, and in particular to Judith Hannam for her patience, particularly when my deadlines were looming. And also to Vicki Murrell for her attention to detail.

Thank you to Cynthia Inions for her beautiful styling with her mountains of ribbons and reams of wrapping paper. To Cath Gratwicke for her utterly beautiful photography and her infectious laughter. And to Rashna Mody Clark for pulling all the elements together so stylishly.

A huge thank you to James and Jo for their never-ending support, encouragement, and hospitality.

But most of all I'd like to thank my parents for instilling in me a passion for food and a love of life.

And to Mungo, who can't read or cook, but gives every recipe his special seal of approval.